THE COLLECTOR'S BOOK OF BOTTLES

Marian Klamkin

THE COLLECTOR'S

BOOKS BY MARIAN KLAMKIN

FLOWER ARRANGING FOR PERIOD DECORATION
FLOWER ARRANGEMENTS THAT LAST
THE COLLECTOR'S BOOK OF ART NOUVEAU
THE COLLECTOR'S BOOK OF BOTTLES
THE COLLECTOR'S BOOK OF BOXES
THE COLLECTOR'S BOOK OF WEDGWOOD

BOOK OF BOTTLES

Illustrated with photographs by Charles Klamkin

DODD, MEAD & COMPANY · NEW YORK

CREDITS FOR PHOTOGRAPHS

Rebner: Mr. and Mrs. Paul Rebner
Watkins: William H. Watkins
Hardy: Mrs. Marjorie Hardy
Mattatuck: Mattatuck Museum
Calabrese: Dan Calabrese
Curulla: Mr. and Mrs. Ernest Curulla
Cross: Mrs. Charlotte Cross
Palmieri: Mr. and Mrs. Anthony Palmieri
Marie Whitney Antiques
National Society of Colonial Dames of America in Connecticut, Webb House

ACKNOWLEDGMENTS

I would like to express my gratitude to Mr. William H. Watkins, Director of the Mattatuck Museum in Waterbury, Connecticut, for permission to photograph the John Prince Elton collection of American Glass bottles and flasks.

I would also like to thank all others whose bottles appear on the following pages, especially Mr. and Mrs. Paul Rebner who were most helpful in placing at our disposal their collection of bottles and source material. Others who deserve special thanks are Mr. Paul Gartzman, Mrs. Marjorie Hardy, and Miss Susan Finlay.

ISBN 0-396-06358-6
Library of Congress Catalog Card Number: 74-158343
Printed in the United States of America

Contents

THE COLLECTOR'S BOOK OF BOTTLES

Chapter 1

THE HOBBY OF BOTTLE COLLECTING

THE phenomenon of the growth of bottle collecting as a hobby is fairly recent and peculiarly American. It is only within the past ten years that interest in gathering old bottles and even many new ones has mushroomed to the extent that there are now thousands of serious collectors and hundreds of organizations whose purpose is the discussion, showing, and trading of bottles and bottle information. It is odd, therefore, that interest in old glass and the literature that was published concerning its manufacture did not, until quite recently, lead to much discussion about bottles.

Often historians and antiquarians have less real sense of the true story of a developing people and their environment than collectors. Collectors will put together the bits and pieces of the past long before they are broken, lost, and forgotten. Those objects that antiquarians think of as "junk" often have an historical and social significance that only the passage of time reveals. While decorative glass has been written about in detail throughout this century, the true story of the glass in-

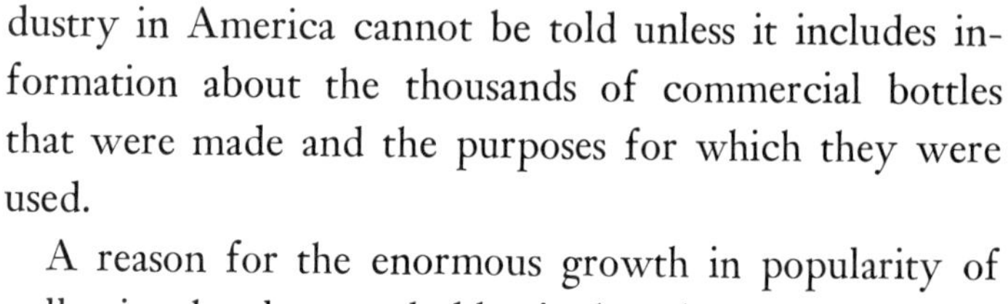

dustry in America cannot be told unless it includes information about the thousands of commercial bottles that were made and the purposes for which they were used.

A reason for the enormous growth in popularity of collecting bottles as a hobby is that there is a category to appeal to everyone. Each category of old bottles conjures up a nostalgia for the past and a better knowledge of the history of our country. The bottle collector's zeal for adding to his collection does not stop when he has acquired the objects he wants. A knowledge of the social habits of past generations and an interest in the economic development of America is as valuable to him as the bottles themselves.

Of necessity, bottle collecting has become an organized hobby. The need to disseminate the vast amount of knowledge necessary to understand the purposes for which many different types of bottles were made and the methods by which they were made is just one reason why bottle collecting clubs have become so popular.

Blob-top light aqua six-sided bottle, blown-in-mold. H. 7 in., c. 1870. Rebner

DR. S. D. HOWE'S
Arabian Tonic Blood Purifier.
Differs from all other preparations in its Immediate Action upon the
Liver, Kidneys and Blood.
Composed of choicest Herbs, Roots and Extracts. Cures Boils, Blotches, Tumors, Salt Rheum, Cancers, Cancerous Humors, Pimples on the Face, Scurvy, Syphilis, Scrofula and all diseases arising from an impure state of the Blood, Malarial Fevers, etc.
For "Nervous Debility," "Lost Vitality," Urinary Diseases" and "Broken Down Constitutions," "I challenge the 19th century" to produce its equal.
Every Bottle is Worth its Weight in Gold.
Price $1 00 per Bottle. Six for $5.00.
Consumption Can Be Cured.
Dr. Howe's Arabian Milk-Cure
Dr. Howe's Arabian Tonic
Dr. Howe's Arabian Liver Pills
The only medicines that have ever been known to "Positively" Cure Consumption.
☞ *CONSUMPTIVES* should use all three preparations with an occasional smoke of the Catarrh Cure.
PRICE—Milk-Cure and Tonic, Each, $1.00. Pills 25c; Catarrh Cure 50c.
Sold by Leavenworth & Dikeman
Druggists, Sole Agents for Waterbury, and
James O. May,
Druggist, Naugatuck, Conn.
DR. S. D. HOWE, Proprietor,
Greenwich St., New York.
f25d&w1y

LEFT: *Self-styled "Doctress" could make broad claims for cures in nineteenth century. Advertising poster offers hope to the sick.* Mattatuck

RIGHT: *Advertisement for medicine sold in 1880. This type of advertisement occurs frequently in late nineteenth-century newspapers.*

Constant exchange of information is desirable if many old bottles are to be properly identified. Glass, perhaps more than any other material, is difficult to place geographically. There have been so many bottles made in so many places in America over the past two hundred years that new information constantly turns up to make bottle collecting a growing and fascinating hobby.

Bottle collectors are America's grass-roots historians. They know that an early Coca-Cola bottle has as important a place in the story of American glass as an eighteenth-century Stiegel perfume flask. They can see

Dr. T. D. DOUGHERTY'S
CELEBRATED
COUGH SYRUP

IS A SURE CURE for Coughs, Colds, Hoarseness, Asthma, Bronchitis, Croup, Lung Fever, Pneumonia, Hemorrhage of the Lungs and all Throat and Lung Diseases. To Consumptives it is invaluable. Three doses will cure an ordinary Cough.
Price 50c and $1 per bottle; sold by all druggists.
T. F. DOUGHERTY, Proprietor,
s1d6m P. O. Box 520, Waterbury, Conn.

LEFT: *Amber embossed bottle for Munyan's "Paw-Paw," a germicide solution. H 10 in., c. 1870.* Rebner

RIGHT: *Many medicines were sold through the newspaper promotions which were mild by today's standards.*
Mattatuck

the point at which an object becomes an artifact and are somewhat less interested in artistic value than in the historic value of their bottles.

In a century where we are as much a pawn of the pitchman as our ancestors were, it is interesting that a majority of the bottles collected today once held mystery liquids that thousands of people believed would perform medical miracles. Euphoria-producing medicines were sold by the gallons in the nineteenth century, and there were few people who did not believe that they would be made well by drinking them. In a developing and busy democracy, where so many truths have been learned by long periods of trial and error, it is perhaps not too difficult to understand why hundreds of thousands of people believed that alcoholic bitters would cure the many ills for which science had as yet found no cure.

One may be tolerant of our forefathers when one realizes that the greatest number of old bottles found today once held alcohol or narcotics. One can only be amazed that so much of importance was acomplished in a nation that must have been at least slightly squiffy much of the time.

While this is probably no less true today than it was a hundred years ago, we are at least aware, when we purchase alcoholic drinks, of what we are getting. It was not until the Pure Food and Drug Laws were passed in 1906 that a teetotaler knew for certain that he was not also an alcoholic. The medicine that he swigged in private for many real and invented diseases was often a stronger drink than the town drunk consumed at the local bar.

By far the greatest number of old bottles collected today held alcohol in one form or another. The American liquor industry as well as foreign distillers and bottlers have known that to most drinkers one whiskey was as good as another, and historically have made an effort to package their products in appealing bottles. This is even more true today than it was in the past. New liquor bottles that will appeal to collectors are

Bottles have been made in thousands of figural shapes and this has become an interesting category for collectors. This medium blue "violin" flask is pontilled and mold-blown. H. 9½ in., c. 1870. Mattatuck

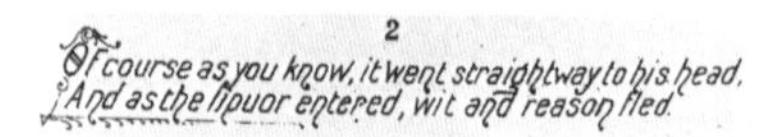

constantly being issued. Not only the whiskey industry, but the glass and ceramics industries, are profiting from the enormous number of bottle collectors who seem to know about new limited-edition bottles before they are even issued. The law of supply and demand makes some of these novelty bottles increase in value within a very short time.

Another factor that helps to account for the popularity of bottle collecting is that it can be happily combined with the hobby of camping. Bottles, old ones, can still be had for the digging and the emergence of camping as a new form of family recreation has led to people discovering old settlements and dumps where bottles and other relics are being dug with an avidity that approximates the Gold Rush of 1849. In the West a mass excavation, often very rewarding, of ghost towns is being carried out to search for old bottles. Collectors who live in the East are no less avid in their search for bottles in the soil, but it is often more difficult.

LEFT: *Figural of man with dog at his side made in clear glass. Embossed "C.I.D." on base. H. 12 in., c. 1875.*
Mattatuck

RIGHT: *Related material such as this late nineteenth-century advertising trade card is sought by bottle collectors.*
Mattatuck

On the following pages I have attempted to document a cross-section of the millions of bottles that have been made in the past and that are being made today that are of interest to collectors. As information about bottles becomes more accessible, there will obviously be more organized groups dedicated to sorting out all the information that can be found concerning the bottles themselves, and the reasons for which they were made. By design, there has been no attempt to choose only those bottles that are especially rare or difficult to find, although many are included in the illustrations.

All bottles illustrated were photographed as they are and no embossments have been painted or otherwise retouched. Therefore, each flask and bottle appears exactly as it is, since it is felt that the novice collector should be able to learn about bottles by looking at the best natural illustrations possible. One category of bottles that is not treated separately is figural bottles, but those who collect these bottles that, for many years, have been

LEFT: *There is an enormous variety of bottles from which the collector may choose. This carved jade snuff bottle was made in China in the nineteenth century. H. 2¾ in.*
Hardy

RIGHT: *The label on this whittle-marked aqua bottle reads, "Water taken from the River Jordan, June, '76," H. 7½ in.*
Mattatuck

made to look like something other than bottles, will find many among other categories.

Many times a collector will want to photograph bottles in his collection or items he may come upon in his travels and cannot acquire. Photographs can be extremely useful in the exchange of information among collectors, in offering a bottle for sale or just to have a record for historical or insurance purposes.

Good, clear photographs can be taken of bottles with a minimum of experience or elaborate equipment. Whether you use a Polaroid, Instamatic or a more sophisticated camera, the basic criteria are the same.

First, avoid using a confusing background. Photograph your bottle against either a well-pressed white cloth or a large sheet of white cardboard or heavy paper. If a suitable background material is not available, you may photograph a bottle in front of an unobstructed large windowpane as long as the background that can be seen through the window is uncluttered.

Second, get as close to the object being photographed

ABOVE: *Primitive glass has appeal for many collectors. This "black" glass bottle with many bubbles caught in the glass could have held beer, mineral water, soda or whiskey. H. 10 in., c. 1850.* Rebner

RIGHT: *Identifying mysterious bottle and jar forms holds a fascination for many collectors. This is a battery jar of type used in the late nineteenth century.* Rebner

as possible. For Polaroids and Instamatics, a portrait or close-up attachment would be a worthwhile investment. For cameras with more precise focusing arrangements try to fill as much of the frame as possible and focus critically on the front of the bottle.

As for lighting, stay away from direct sunlight falling on the bottle, since it will produce distracting reflections and shadows. Photograph in open shade or if you are using an artificial light or flash, bounce it off a white reflector such as a piece of cardboard, a wall or ceiling.

Modern, high-speed photographic films, whether black-and-white or color, are quite capable of producing a good image without using strong, bright sunlight directly on the subject.

Obviously, photographing a dark bottle against a light background is not much of a problem. However, in order to photograph a clear bottle and still be able to distinguish the embossing requires a little more care. For this type of bottle an additional light source should be employed. You do not need professional spotlights, pho-

The imperfect form of early bottles is part of their charm. This mid-nineteenth-century decanter has hand-applied, crooked neck. Mattatuck

Collecting miniature bottles is yet another interesting category in which one may specialize. Miniature demijohn on left is light aqua with a kick-up base and rough pontil. Bottle on right has basketweave surface. H. 2¾ in.
Hardy

tofloods or movie "sun-guns." An ordinary 100-watt household bulb held to the side of the bottle will accent the raised lettering so that it can be made legible.

Do not be afraid to use color film. Whether you are producing color prints or slides you will find that the detail will be surprisingly good even with those clear, embossed bottles that are so hard to photograph. Just remember to use the kind of film that is made for the type of light you are using. Daylight film should be used when shooting outdoors and indoor film when using artificial light.

There are bottles that appeal to every collector's instinct. Many are amusing or have amusing histories. Some are magnificently made and colored and others are primitive and made of the coarsest glass and have appeal for those reasons. For those who prefer pottery or porcelain to glass, there are many bottles from which to choose. The historian will find a wealth of information embossed on old bottles, but for the nostalgic, bottle collecting can bring a lifetime of pleasure.

Chapter 2

HOW BLOWN BOTTLES ARE MADE

IT is important for anyone who collects old bottles to understand the nature of glass, the materials from which it is made and how it is shaped and finished. Armed with this knowledge it will be a fairly simple matter for the bottle collector to identify the age and origin of specimens.

The ingredients in glass are mainly silica (sand or quartz), carbonate of soda and/or lime. When lead oxides are added glass becomes harder, more brilliant, and is what we call crystal or flint glass. Soda-lime glass is the oldest known type of glass made and its natural colors are green shading to brown. It is light in weight and usually has impurities obvious to the naked eye. Soda-lime glass was improved by adding potassium during and after the fifteenth century, and it is clearer and freer of blemishes. Potassium-soda-lime glass was made throughout the eighteenth century in America.

An improved soda-lime glass was used in this country in the nineteenth century and perhaps it is this glass that chiefly concerns bottle collectors. Soda-lime glass reflects

the light from the surface. Flint glass, an invention attributed to George Ravenscroft of England, has been made for two hundred years and when compared with soda-lime glass is more brilliant, harder, clearer of color, and without imperfections. Flint glass reflects the light internally. While flint glass has been used for decorative glass, soda-lime glass was commonly used for bottle manufacture. An improved soda-lime glass that was first made in America is attributed to a Mr. Leighton of West Virginia and dates from the end of the Civil War.

Additional materials used in glass making give the glass its color. Nickel, silver, copper or iron will turn glass green. Gold, copper or selenium are used to make glass red. Uranium, gold or chromium will turn glass yellow, and cobalt is used to make blue glass. Phosphates or fluorides of calcium are used to obtain opal effects, tin or calcium to make white glass, and the addition of manganese or nickel will give shades ranging from purple to black. These materials are often used in combination to achieve various shades and colors in glass. Arsenic is

OPPOSITE

LEFT: *Simple free-blown bottle of green glass, very bubbled. Rough pontil. H. 5 in.* Mattatuck

RIGHT: *"Ludlow" or "chestnut" bottle in light aqua glass. Shape was made for over a hundred years. H. 9 in.* Rebner

Early nineteenth - century whiskey flask in dark green glass made at Keene, New Hampshire, Glass Works. H 6¾ in. Mattatuck

sometimes added to glass metal to eliminate bubbles.

There are three methods used to shape glass. It may be blown, pressed or molded. It is important for the bottle collector to be able to recognize the properties of bottles made by these three different methods of shaping. Glass is a liquid and the ingredients of which it is made are melted together to form a substance which, as it cools, may be given any one of a number of shapes.

The invention of the blowpipe dates back to ancient times. Throughout several thousand years of bottle production, the same simple method of attaching a blob of hot glass to the end of a hollow tube has been used. The blowpipe is the most essential tool of the glassblower and it was not replaced with mechanized equipment until the beginning of this century.

It is not our purpose here to describe, step by step, the process used for making glass bottles. However, the collector has to know something about the methods used and, what is even more important, the tools used for shaping bottles, since he wants to be able to recognize the old mouth-blown bottles for which he and his fellow enthusiasts have a passion.

Once the sand and other ingredients are placed in the crucible or clay melting pot, they are heated to melting point. The mixture becomes a syrupy liquid not unlike a batch of grape jelly that has reached its proper temperature. Molten glass also has some of the other properties of grape jelly when it is cooking. As it is heated it collects foam on the top and many bubbles throughout. Like jelly, the molten glass must be skimmed and gradually cooled. The process of cooling, or annealing, is extremely important to the quality of the glass.

When a glass batch has reached its proper temperature a heated blowpipe is dipped into it and turned until enough of the liquid adheres to the end of the blowpipe. This blob of molten sand is called a gather or post. The gather is then rolled on a marble or metal slab (the marver) until it is round and even. Meanwhile the glassblower has already begun to blow into the pipe to form a bubble in the center of the gather. Once the

Washington whiskey flask that was improperly cooled in the process of being annealed. Note dent in shoulder of reverse. c. 1825. Mattatuck

Open pontil scar on flask made in two-part mold.

bubble is started the gather becomes a parison and the blower continues to blow and rotate the metal until it is the proper size and shape.

The second most important tool for the glassblower is the pontil rod (or pontee or puntee). This is a long rod which, after being dipped into a hot pot of glass metal, is used to hold the blown bottle when it is removed from the blowpipe. The pontil rod is attached at the top of the bubble which becomes the bottom of the finished bottle. When the pontil rod is attached a few drops of cold water are applied to the end of the blowpipe, the neck of the bottle is tapped slightly and the blowpipe broken off. The bottle is then reheated and the neck is trimmed. The pontil rod is then broken off, leaving a small round rough scar on the base of the bottle. This is the method used to make the most simple and primitive kind of useful bottle. Other tools that are used in the process of shaping a free-blown bottle are the pucella, a scissors-like tool with blades of charred wood; shears; a trowel for shaping the parison; and a battledore, a wooden paddle for shaping the sides of the bottle.

The above process is also used when a bottle is shaped in a mold, except that the parison is blown into the mold and blown some more until the bubble has expanded to reach the sides of the mold. A discussion of the various kinds of molds used in shaping bottles in the eighteenth and nineteenth centuries will be treated separately, since it is necessary to understand the various molds used in order to date bottles and identify their method of manufacture.

Once the free-blown bottle has been broken from the blowpipe there are several methods of finishing it off. The bottle might be placed into the annealing oven and left a short while. This gives the surface of the glass a high polish. Towards the end of the nineteenth century a separate oven called the glory hole was used for this finishing process. The glory hole was kept at a higher temperature than the annealing oven and glass made by this method had a very high polish.

Glass must be cooled gradually to prevent the metal

OPPOSITE PAGE
LEFT: *Ring-shaped pontil scar.*

RIGHT: *Ground pontil on free-blown bottle.*

Bare iron pontil on turn-mold bottle.

from exploding and therefore, the bottle was placed in a special oven or in a cooler part of the kiln. After the bottle had gradually cooled it was ready for the market. Various methods of shaping the lip of the bottle will be discussed later.

When a bottle was made by the above method, without a mold, no two bottles could be identical in shape. Although the glassblower was highly skilled, these bottles required the cooperation of several apprentices and helpers. It is the knowledge of the process and methods used to make early free-blown, or "off-hand," bottles that makes these primitive, but practical, glass bubbles the most highly prized items in many glass collections.

RIGHT: *Blown-in-mold bottle with zinc screw cap. Seam to top of shoulder indicates bottle was made before 1860.* Rebner

BELOW RIGHT: *Green glass bottle with rough surface, or "whittle marks," made by blowing into cold mold.* Rebner

LEFT: *Light golden amber decanter, pattern-molded. Of type made in Zanesville, Ohio, in mid-nineteenth century. H. 8 in.* Mattatuck

Chapter 3

BOTTLE MOLDS, MOLD MARKS, AND CLOSURES FOR BOTTLES

AN old bottle will tell its own story of when it was made and by what method. To the bottle collector, mold and seam marks quite easily identify bottles to have been made within a certain period of time. Other criteria, of course, have to be taken into account as well, since bottles are still being made in various parts of the world by the free-blown or blown-in-mold methods.

Mold or seam marks are found where sections of a hinged mold join together. It was necessary for there to be some space between the sections of the mold for air to escape as the bottle was being blown. Otherwise, as the glass was being forced into the mold the replaced air would cause the glass to form a pocket of air inside the mold. Since these mold seams exist, it is almost always possible to tell what kind of mold was used.

The use of molds in bottle making is an ancient method of shaping bottles. However, for the purposes of the bottle collector, the important period of mold design began in the seventeenth century when the hinged brass mold was first developed. The iron mold was made a

Sheared neck found on earliest bottles. Closure was cork.

hundred years later. American glassmakers continued to make bottles by the free-blown method long after European bottle manufacturers used molds. The free-blown bottle will, of course, have no seam or mold marks.

The use of molds had enormous advantages for glassblowers of nineteenth-century America. Bottles could be made that were uniform in size and shape. Various surface patterns and designs could be used and as mold making and design improved, embossed advertising could be blown into the surface of bottles cheaply enough to make personalized bottles for the growing industries that needed them.

The first molds to be used in this country shaped only the bottom two-thirds of the bottle, and the shoulders and neck required hand-shaping once the glass was removed from the mold. The non-shoulder one-piece mold was a cylinder that was slightly larger in circumference at the top in order to facilitate removal of the glass from the mold.

The two types of non-shoulder molds used by Ameri-

LEFT: *Flared neck made with glassblower's tools.*

BELOW: *Rolled collar.*

can glassmakers were the smooth mold which gave no distinctive pattern to the glass, and the pattern mold which had designs cut into the inner surface. Patterns such as ridges, roped designs, diamonds, etc. were formed on the surface of the glass when it was blown into these molds. Often the bottle was removed from the pattern mold and blown further to expand the pattern which remained in the glass. Another method of further decoration was to remove the parison, redip it in molten glass, and place it in a second mold that was slightly larger than the first. This is called the German half-post method of molding glass. Since the second dipping did not cover the surface farther than the shoulders of the bottle, these bottles are easily identifiable. One can detect the place near the neck where the second layer of glass ends.

Shoulder-height molds that were hinged were also used in the early part of the nineteenth century. The advantage of a mold that opened up for removal of the bottle was that the mold was not tapered and embossments of a more complicated nature could be used. A

LEFT: *Single applied collar.*

RIGHT: *Double applied collar.*

larger variety of shapes was possible with the hinged shoulder-height mold. A bottle made in the shoulder-height hinged mold will have seams extending around the shoulder of the bottle and one seam up either side. The neck will have no seams since it was hand-tooled.

The other basic type of mold, of which there are many variations, is the full-height mold. One variation is the bottom-hinged mold which will make a bottle with a seam across the bottom. This seam might be partly obliterated by the pontil scar. Seams run up both sides of these bottles. This type of mold was also called a clamshell mold. The side seams run up the neck about half way and the mouth of the bottle was still formed by hand.

The full-height three-part dip mold included the round cannister-type bottom section and a two-section hinged mold that formed the top of the bottle. This type of mold made it possible for embossments to be made on the upper part of the bottle. Seams on a bottle made in the three-part dip mold will run horizontally around the

shoulder, from which two seams will run upwards toward the lip.

The three (or more)-part leaf mold had vertical sections that were hinged at the sides. Two of these sections could be opened up to allow for easy removal of the bottle. The sections were attached to a bottom plate that formed the base of the bottle. Many of the decorative decanters made in the early part of the nineteenth century were made in leaf molds, but this type of mold was seldom used for commercial bottles.

Another variation of the shoulder-height mold was the post-bottom mold. A metal post centered the bottle in the mold and caused an indentation in the bottom of the bottle. Bottles made in this type of leaf mold will have a round seam on the base of the bottle. A cup-bottom mold in which the centering base is depressed in the bottom plate will make a seam running horizontally near the base of the bottle.

Another type of mold to consider is the full-height blow-back mold which leaves seams that run vertically

LEFT: *Blob top bottle. Wire wound around neck held cork in place.*

RIGHT: *Codd marble stopper bottle patented in 1872-3.*

to the top of the bottle. In this mold the entire bottle, including the lip, was formed in the mold.

The above methods for shaping bottles were all used in the nineteenth century. It was not until the end of that century that Michael J. Owens invented an automatic bottle-making machine that speeded the process of bottle manufacture and eliminated the need for skilled glassblowers.

The earliest automatic bottle machine bottles are sought by collectors, but those mouth-blown bottles made before 1900 are the most desirable.

Evidence that a bottle was made by the process of mouth-blowing can be detected by clues other than seam marks. Pontil scars and sheared mouths are two features of early bottles for which the collector looks. There will be some bottles that will show no seams, but will be smooth, round, and uniform. Many bottles, particularly those used for wine, were turned in the mold, a process which obliterated the seams and polished the surface of

Hutchinson-type closure invented by Charles G. Hutchinson in 1879 is made of rubber gasket wired between two metal discs.

the glass. A turn-mold bottle has striations running horizontally around the bottle surface.

Whittle marks can be found on many old bottles and were caused by the bottle being put into molds which were not hot enough. Some of the bottles showing whittle marks were made in wood molds which were carved and not as smooth as metal.

Various types of tool scars can be found on old bottles, one, of course, being the pontil scar. Pontil scars were removed in most cases from decorative glass objects by grinding, but they were left on the inexpensive commercial bottles. At times the remaining glass scar is so rough and jagged that an old bottle will not stand upright on a shelf.

A ring-shaped pontil mark will be left when a blowpipe is used in place of the pontil rod. The glassblower, working alone rather than with an assistant, would detach his blowpipe from the neck of the bottle and quickly attach it to the bottom. This required skill since the blow-

Lightning stopper, invented in 1875. This one is porcelain for pottery bottle.

pipe had to be moved rapidly before it was too cool to adhere to the glass.

Another method of pontilling did not use the usual method of a hot blob of glass on the end of the iron rod. Instead, the end of the rod was heated until very hot and pressed directly on to the base of the bottle. The tip of this rod was flared and the center had a circular indentation. This method left a smoother scar since no wafer of glass was applied. The rod also left another mark—the oxidized iron of the pontil rod around the base of the bottle.

Shortly after the bare iron pontil was developed, another and more convenient method for holding the hot glass was invented. The snap, a holder that gripped the bottle on either side while the base of the bottle was braced against a cup-shaped bottom, was developed after the middle of the nineteenth century. Until the development of the automatic bottle-making machine, the snap was used to hold the bottle while it was being detached from the blowpipe. One can sometimes find an old

Lightning stopper for soda or beer.

bottle with no pontil scar, but with small scars on either side where it was held by the snap.

Other characteristics of old bottles are: stretch marks where the neck of the bottle has been drawn up and shaped; applied lips of various types; and various imperfections in the glass, the most desirable of all being the trapped air bubbles that are characteristic of the early soda-lime glass.

An important development in mold making during the latter half of the nineteenth century was the invention of the plate mold. This made it possible for glass bottle manufacturers to make standard shaped and sized bottles that could be made cheaply with embossed lettering. Instead of having to design a new mold for each customer, a plate could be inserted in the standard mold. The plate could be made to order cheaply and this made it possible for the small customer to have personalized molds. Customers who needed large quantities of bottles of one size usually had complete molds made.

The plate mold is important for the collector of the

Inside screw thread closure.

Crown cap closure invented by William Painter in 1891.

many commercial bottles of the latter half of the nineteenth century. Since even the small corner druggist could afford to have his own plate designed, there are literally thousands of different embossments to be found on bottles of this period. It is sometimes possible to ascertain whether a product was sold in large quantities or not, when it was the smaller user who had plate-mold bottles for his products. Bottles collected from this period are prized for their interesting, amusing or informative embossments, but it is unlikely that such a variety would be available for the collector were it not for the development of the plate mold.

Chapter 4

THE DEVELOPMENT OF THE AMERICAN GLASS INDUSTRY

IN the story of American glass, commercial bottles always play a secondary role. Yet it is doubtful that glass making as an industry would have become so important to the American economy without the development of bottle manufacture in the eighteenth and nineteenth centuries. Many of the manufacturers of decorative glass depended upon their sales of inexpensive bottles to support the fussier work required to develop other glass objects.

There is sufficient evidence to believe that industrial glass making was carried on in America long before the Revolutionary War. Records show that a glass house was built in Jamestown, Virginia, at the beginning of the seventeenth century. Glassmakers were imported from Holland, Germany, Italy, and Poland, and two necessary items, window glass and bottles, were made. Glass beads, used for trading with the Indians, are also thought to be an early product of Jamestown. The Jamestown glass house was not commercially successful. There were many other attempts to make glass during the seventeenth cen-

RIGHT: *Stiegel-type bottle enameled in conventionalized floral design in bright colors.* National Society of Colonial Dames of America in Connecticut. Webb House

BELOW: *Clear glass decanter with hand-applied gold grape and tendril design. Probably European.* Mattatuck

tury in various other colonial settlements. Glass was made in Salem, Massachusetts, New York, and Philadelphia. However, there are few records from which products of these glass houses can be identified.

The problem of attribution continues to plague scholars even when eighteenth-century production is being discussed. Even the major glass houses that were developed and which endured through a large part of the eighteenth century have rather sketchy histories. The first glass house of importance about which there is some information is that of Caspar Wistar, who built his enterprise in Salem County, New Jersey, in 1739. Wistar, a button-maker from Philadelphia, brought men from Germany to teach the art of glassmaking to himself and his son. The chief products turned out by this firm were off-hand ordinary green glass bottles and window glass. The Wistar glass house continued in production, at first under Caspar's direction and then under the direction of his son, Richard, until shortly after the Revolutionary War.

Other eighteenth-century glass houses were established in New York and Massachusetts in the pre-Revolutionary War period. These establishments, also, depended upon their output of free-blown bottles and window glass for support. Since there was little difference in the quality of this early production between one glass house and another or European glass of the same type, there is no way to distinguish American bottles of this period.

Henry William Stiegel was the first glassmaker in America to make bottles that could be distinguished from other American bottles of the same period. Stiegel was a German immigrant who opened his first glass house in Lancaster, Pennsylvania, in 1763. Stiegel's bottles so resembled many that were made in Europe at the same time that it is all but impossible to tell whether existing bottles made in the Stiegel tradition are, in fact, from his factory. It has become customary, therefore, to identify all old bottles that were made in the shapes, styles, and colors of Stiegel production as "Stiegel-type" bottles. This arbitrary method of classifying old American glass made in

ABOVE: *South Jersey-type flask in light aqua with white loopings. H. 7⅛ in.* Mattatuck

LEFT: *European glass picnic flask with applied loopings on edges. Light aqua. H. 4½ in.* Mattatuck

RIGHT: *Stiegel-type cornflower blue flask has petalled flower incised on base over pontil mark. H. 5½ in.* Mattatuck

BELOW: *This bright cornflower blue flask may be European. Flared mouth, pontil mark. H. 8 in.* Mattatuck

a certain recognizable tradition is also used in connection with other glass firms. The problem is further complicated because glassblowers were an itinerant lot, so that bottles were blown in the Stiegel tradition in the other new glass houses that were opened up. However, the beautiful expand-mold scent bottles and enameled or etched decanters attributed to Stiegel are becoming so scarce and expensive that it makes little difference to the collector that their attribution cannot be determined exactly.

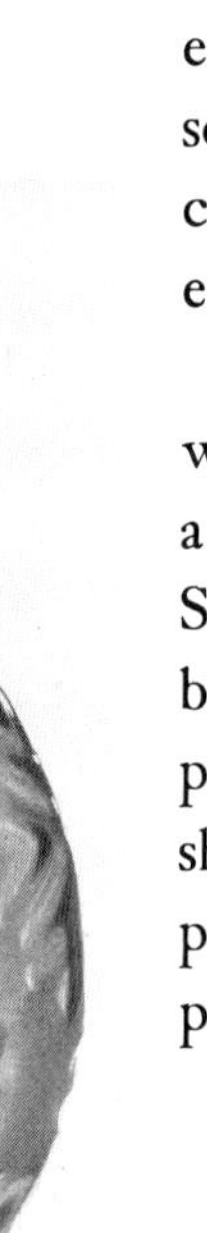

The career of Henry William Stiegel as a glassmaker was short and prolific, but it thoroughly destroyed him as a businessman. After having built three glass houses, Stiegel became bankrupt in 1774. High living and poor business judgement in over-expanding during a difficult period in the nation's history, put an end to Stiegel's short-lived career in the glass business, and he died a pauper in 1785 after having served a term in debtor's prison.

The bottles that have been attributed to the glass

LEFT: *Small pocket flask, Stiegel-type, is ribbed vertically, ribs twisted at neck. Dark amber. H. 4¾ in.* Mattatuck

RIGHT: *Large flask has pattern of vertical ribs, twisted at neck. Dark amber. H. 7¾ in.* Mattatuck

LEFT: *Dark green pocket flask with broken rib pattern. H. 6½ in.* Mattatuck

RIGHT: *Small amber Stiegel-type pocket flask has ribs swirled to right. H. 4¾ in.* Mattatuck

houses owned by Stiegel are varied. They range from the Nile green household bottles to the decorative pattern-molded and expanded pocket scent bottles in jewel-like shades of blue and amethyst. Patterns used for these bottles are diamond-daisy, diamond-diaper, daisy-in-hexagon, and various ribbed and quilted patterns. The pocket bottles have sheared necks. Other bottles listed in the account books of the Manheim Glass Works are: "Quart decanters, molded; Quart decanters, plain; Pint and half pint decanters, plain; Smelling bottles; Junk bottles; Cruets; Phials and other bottles for Chymists and Apothecaries; Ink bottles; Wide-mouthed bottles for sweetmeats."

Another eighteenth-century glass house of which little has been recorded, but which is important since so much work of a particular style has been attributed to it, is the Pitkin Glass Works, founded by William and Elisha Pitkin and Samuel Bishop in Manchester, Connecticut, in 1783. The Pitkin Glass Works remained in business until around 1830. Small flasks, made by the German half-post

OPPOSITE PAGE
LEFT: *Cornflower blue ribbed pocket flask. Glass is very bubbled. H. 6¾ in.* Mattatuck

RIGHT: *Pitkin-type flask, dark green, ribs swirled to right. Made by German half-post method. H. 7¼ in.* Mattatuck

Pitkin-type flask, medium green, with vertical and swirled ribs. H. 7 in. Mattatuck

method, have long been attributed to this firm. These flasks are in olive-amber, amber, and olive-green and many of them were made in a swirl pattern or variations thereof. Regardless of the fact that other glass houses were known to have made similar pocket flasks, the name "Pitkin flask" has been the identifying term for these bottles, and a great many flasks of this type have been found in Connecticut for many years. Because these flasks cannot be attributed with certainty to the one glass house, they are now referred to as "Pitkin-type" flasks.

By the turn of the century there were many other glass houses being established throughout New England, in New York, New Jersey, and West to Ohio. Few bottles can definitely be ascribed to a particular house and certain types of bottles are identified as being of the "South Jersey-type" or "Ohio-type." After the Revolutionary War the glass industry fell upon difficult times: there were many openings and closings of glass houses, and workers migrated from one area to another. This makes absolute identification of bottles made during this period an impossible task. It is only in the nineteenth century, when the whiskey industry kept the glass fires burning by purchasing huge quantities of historical and pictorial flasks, that we can find some marked bottles of definite attribution.

ABOVE: *Pitkin-type pocket flask, dark amber, with vertical and swirled ribs. H. 5½ in.* Mattatuck

RIGHT: *Stiegel-type light aqua pocket flask in quilted design. H. 5½ in.* Mattatuck

BOTTOM: *Stiegel-type pocket flask; pattern-molded and expanded design of small diamonds above 28 vertical flutes. Deep amethyst color. Glass very bubbled. H. 5 in.* Mattatuck

Chapter 5

DR. DYOTT AND HIS FLASKS

TO devotees of American glass whiskey bottles, the most highly prized are the historical and pictorial flasks made during the first half of the nineteenth century. Although the last flasks of this type were made around 1860, it wasn't until the 1920s that they were recognized as uniquely American and valued as collectors' items. A great many of these flasks were made and they have been credited with having made a major contribution toward the financial solvency of some of the glass houses of the period. Since historical and pictorial flasks were collected early in this century, many have found their way to museums, but others, from private collections, are just recently coming on the market.

Masonic flasks with the American eagle were made as early as 1816 in Keene, New Hampshire, and the following year similar flasks were made in East Hartford, Connecticut. However, the first historical flasks that have been recorded in detail and about which there is enough recorded information for easy identification are those manufactured by Thomas W. Dyott, proprietor of the

Flask made at Kensington Glass Works. Dr. Dyott's initials on reverse. Washington in uniform, three-quarters view facing to left. Aqua. Plain lip, pontil mark. H. 7 in.
Mattatuck

Kensington Glass Works of Philadelphia. The earliest advertisements for Dyott's flasks are dated 1822. Eighteen flasks of this year were described and can be identified from the records of the glass works that he owned.

Thomas W. Dyott is one of the most colorful figures in the history of American glass bottle manufacture. Evidently a self-styled Doctor of Medicine, as were many druggists and purveyors of patent medicines of the period, Dyott settled in Philadelphia in 1805. Selling his cures for syphilis and other ailments at high profits, this British-born druggist became very successful within a few years. The widespread sale of Dr. Dyott's medicines required many vials and bottles.

Adequate supplies of glass bottles were a problem for Dr. Dyott. The War of 1812 had cut off supplies of British-made glass and American manufacturers were not geared to make the quantity nor the quality of bottles that Dr. Dyott wanted. In 1815 Dr. Dyott acquired an interest in the Olive Glass Works at Glassboro, New Jersey. Concurrent with this investment, Dyott's business expanded to become a wholesale and retail establishment which dealt in many diversified commodities.

By 1818 Dr. Dyott had acquired the glassworks outside of Philadelphia in which his first historical flasks were made. Six years later he advertised Lafayette flasks, one of which he presented to the French war hero when the famous entourage came to Philadelphia. Dyott's glassworks also made Ben Franklin, George Washington, cornucopia, agricultural, and Masonic flasks. On two of the Ben Franklin flasks, Dr. Dyott had his own picture embossed on the reverse. On others, his initials, T. W. D., are used.

Dr. Dyott had several serious business reverses during his career, the last of which sent him to prison. However, before this was to happen, he had created an entire village at Kensington which he called Dyottville. Dyottville was organized in the early 1830s and was a model community whose sole purpose was the business of glass making. Houses, stores, stables, laundries, and carpentershops were built to accommodate the employees who all lived

Masonic flask with farmer's tools and sheaf of wheat inside Masonic arch and pavement. Reverse is ship, Franklin, *"Free Trade and Sailors' Rights," and Kensington Glass Works embossed around ribs. Pale aqua. H. 6¾ in.* Mattatuck

Flask made at Dyottville. Obverse: "The Father of His Country" and classical profile of Washington. Reverse: "General Taylor Never Surrenders," and profile of Zachary Taylor in uniform. Pale aqua. H. 5½ in.

Mattatuck

by rules set down by their employer. Thought to be a model community of its type, Dyottville had many innovative features, and apprentices and employees were all treated with respect and fairness. Hours and working conditions were humane when compared to other industrial communities of this type. Due to unfortunate banking investments Dr. Dyott was only to control his own town for five years.

Thousands of flasks with portraits, eagles, Masonic emblems, and other patriotic motifs were made at Kensington from molds designed especially for this glass firm. Other smaller glass houses bought molds from firms that specialized in mold making.

Portrait and historical flasks were made in full-size two-piece molds in pint and quart sizes. Ordinary bottle glass was used for almost all of these flasks in many shades of aquamarine, green, amber, and sometimes blue. The beautiful amethyst shades of glass that had been used for perfume flasks are seldom seen in the whiskey flasks of the nineteenth century. Hundreds of thousands of this

Columbia flask made at Kensington Glass Works. Obverse: Profile bust of Columbia with cap; "Kensington" embossed below. Reverse: eagle and "Union Co."
Mattatuck

type of spirits flasks were made by glass houses throughout the East and the Midwest. When a flask has some sort of mark such as the name of the glass house that made it or, as in some cases, the initials of the glassmaker, it is, obviously, easy to identify. However, there are many popular flasks that remain impossible to identify as to where they were made or by whom.

Historical and portrait flasks were an important item for American glassmakers and their steady sale through the first half of the nineteenth century did much to keep glass houses in business through trying financial crises. The interest of collectors in these truly American bottles began early in this century and prices of the more common flasks have stabilized somewhat. Of late, the less common flasks have begun to rise in price considerably. As the hobby of bottle collecting grows, the demand for pictorial and historical flasks will continue to increase and it is doubtful whether any other category of bottle collecting would be a better investment. For the student of American history, these flasks are of real interest.

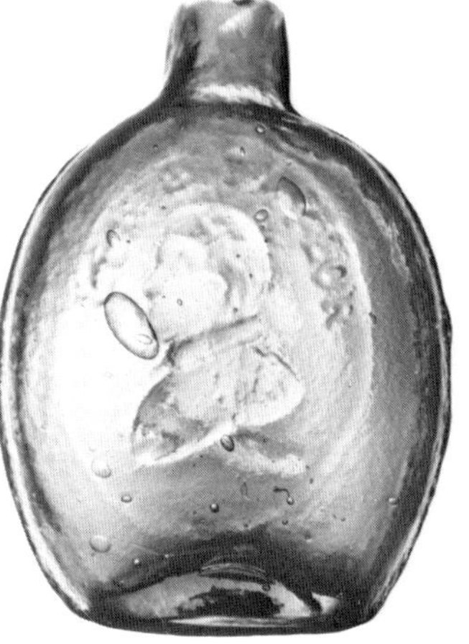

Washington and Taylor flask made at Dyottville Glass Works. Very bubbled, rough surface. Pint capacity.
Mattatuck

Chapter 6

PORTRAITS OF PATRIOTS ON FLASKS

THE popularity of portrait flasks and flasks commemorating national events and sentiments grew to such enormous proportions that it taxed the imaginations of the moldmakers and delighted the customers. The enormous continual sale of these flasks kept many glass houses in business through difficult economic periods, while the prosperity of the whiskey industry also helped.

Although nineteenth-century flasks bearing portraits of famous personages have, in the past, been treated as part of the very large category of "historical" bottles, it might be as well to consider these flasks separately in order to assess their value as an American primitive art form.

The medium of glass blown by mouth into a two-piece mold does not lend itself to the romanticized portrait and the "likenesses" of our great patriots that appear on early flasks are often closer to cartoons than direct likenesses. While the early glassblowers have been extolled for their talent and perseverance in helping to establish a successful American industry against many odds, it is the mold

designer who truly exhibited an interesting talent and art style in his portraiture. While the earlier expand-mold bottles showed some signs of individualistic style, the historical flasks were a manifestation of an American folk-art style that exhibited little or no European influence. All previous American bottles have European prototypes. The historical flasks are American. The portraits are recognizable likenesses done with the use of a few lines. A complete understanding of both glass and metal were necessary for the moldmaker to make a successful design.

It is likely that the inspiration for portrait flasks and, indeed, for all historical flasks, came from the pottery makers of the Staffordshire region of England. In an attempt to recapture the American market for their wares after the War of 1812, these potters decorated plates and pitchers with American patriotic symbols and motifs. A process for printing decoration on plates had been discovered not long before and the medium was ideal for turning out pictorial plates by the thousands cheaply enough to compete with any other ceramics. The added

Washington in uniform. This aqua flask is unusual in that "N" in "General" is backwards. H. 6⅞ in. Mattatuck

appeal to Americans of having scenes from their own country on their plates meant that the British pottery became widely accepted.

In a country that had just fought for and won its freedom, patriotism was extremely strong. What was good for the Staffordshire potters most certainly would be beneficial to struggling American glassmakers who were having a difficult time competing with foreign glasshouses. At that time, as now, alcoholic drink played an important part in American life and a great deal was distilled and consumed. The inspiration to depict the portraits of American patriots on the bottles was an important step in keeping American glass houses in business through the postwar period.

The patriotism that was so rampant following the Revolutionary War and the War of 1812 will probably never be quite as strong again. Communications were slow and in many areas, almost non-existent. Patriotism and its resultant symbols tied the young nation together. The struggling glass industry understood the ready acceptance

"G. Geo. Washington" flask is initialed on reverse side and can therefore be identified as having been made by Frederick Lorenz, Pittsburgh. Clear light green. H. 6¾ in.
Mattatuck

This General Washington flask is of clear glass and and shows Washington three-quarters view facing left. Reverse is initialled "J.R." for John Robinson and "Laird, Sc. Pitt." is embossed around base. Mattatuck

of any chauvinistic symbols and pictures of patriots, when they were portrayed on the containers of the great leveller, whiskey. It was an easy matter to drink toasts to "The Father of our Country" when his profile decorated the whiskey bottle. Drinking could be justified in the name of patriotism when the bottle displayed the new American flag or the belligerent eagle.

George Washington is the subject of more flasks than any other American patriot. Those flasks depicting Washington in uniform were all made between the years 1820 and 1830. In most cases the American eagle is the motif on the reverse of Washington flasks. Those flasks which show Washington in classical bust style are later than the uniformed Washingtons. In profile, the many faces of George Washington seem to have as many different shapes of nose. Yet there is still no doubt that, even without the name surrounding the portraits, we would recognize whose profile it is.

The variations in the manner in which the flasks were identified by the moldmakers is also interesting and amus-

ing. "G. George Washington," "G. G. Washington," "G. Washington," and "Washington" are all used. On later flasks, made mostly in Dyottville and Lockport, New York, "The Father of His Country" is the identifying description. The collector should be aware that the reversal of a letter in the mold makes one flask more collectible than another with the letters the right way round. In all, there are over sixty known "Washington" flasks, any one of which is a find for a collector today.

The majority of Washington flasks are in light aqua color and many of them have similar shapes. Moldmakers changed locations and jobs frequently and many small glass houses purchased their molds from the same moldmaker. The majority of the early Washington flasks were made in the Monongahela and Pittsburgh districts and Kensington near Philadelphia. Some Washington flasks have been attributed to the Dyottville Glass Works and the Lockport Glass Works of Lockport, New York. Many more cannot be attributed at all and probably never will be.

Washington's profile faces left on this flask. The reverse side has a profile of Zachary Taylor and "Bridgeton, New Jersey." Dark aqua. H. 6¾ in. Mattatuck

Washington shares this flask, attributed to Keene, New Hampshire Glass Works, with Andrew Jackson. Amber. H. 6¾ in. Mattatuck

This profile flask of Washington, made by the Albany Glass Works, shows the Baltimore Monument on the reverse side. It is pale amethyst. H. 7¼ in. Mattatuck

Washington flask in dark amber with collared mouth. The reverse shows a full-rigged ship. H. 7⅛ in. Mattatuck

Andrew Jackson flask in medium green. Jackson three-quarters view facing left. Reverse: flowers and foliage in symmetrical design. Attributed to Monongahela and Pittsburgh districts. H. 6¾ in. Mattatuck

Other American patriots who were chosen as models for flask decoration are John Quincy Adams, Andrew Jackson, William Henry Harrison, Zachary Taylor, and Benjamin Franklin. Because of the single purpose of these flasks, to hold spirituous liquors, the moldmakers obviously made no attempt to chronicle all early American historical personages. The purpose for the subject choices seemed to be to design flasks with those patriots who enjoyed the greatest popularity. A barometer of that popularity is the number of flasks made for each of the subjects chosen.

John Quincy Adams, son of our second President, was a great patriot and a man of immense integrity. Yet there is only one known Adams flask. The face of Andrew Jackson, a bitter rival of Adams in the 1825 presidential campaign, adorns at least eight flasks. Jackson, who became President in 1829, was a more colorful personality than his rival and he was a hero to the workingman of the East and to the farmers of the East, West and South.

OPPOSITE PAGE: This Taylor *flask, made in Pittsburgh area, is yellow-aqua. H. $6\frac{3}{8}$ in.*
Mattatuck

This Taylor flask, on which Taylor's head appears to be bald, is light aqua. On reverse, the word "Masterson" appears over eagle. Made in Pittsburgh area. H. $8\frac{1}{2}$ in.
Mattatuck

Obviously, the glassmakers knew which face would sell more whiskey and, therefore, more bottles.

The portrait bust of William Henry Harrison, ninth President of the United States, appears on only one flask. Like Jackson, Harrison was a military hero turned politician. The slogan "The Log Cabin and Hard Cider Candidate" was given to Harrison by the Whig Party during the election campaign. This slogan, a slur on Harrison's attempt to appear poverty-stricken and, therefore, gain the sympathy of the masses, had a reverse effect on the voters. There are two flasks, which were made during this campaign, showing the log cabin and the cider barrel.

There were a great many counterparts of today's campaign button that were given out or sold during Harrison's campaign and the "Hard Cider" flasks were probably among them. The campaign was lively with a lot of premature celebration, and Harrison won the election with a large majority. Again, a hero of the people had captured the imagination of the flask makers.

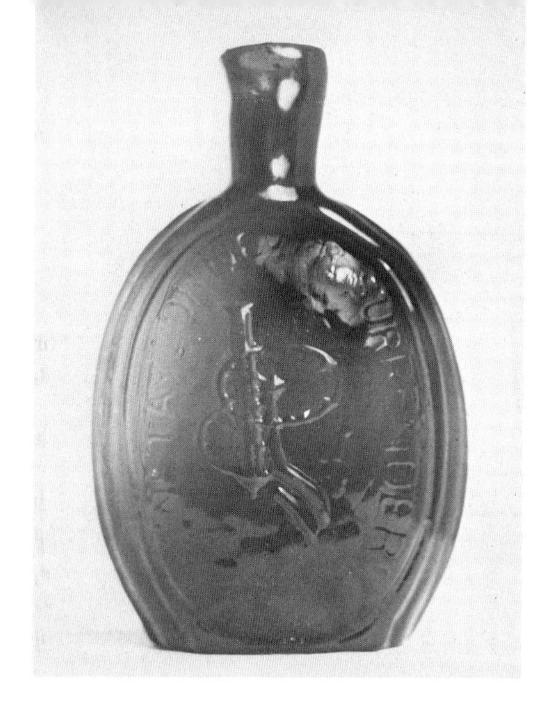

Although no portrait appears on this flask, it commemorates Zachary Taylor. Obverse: cannon mounted on two-wheel carriage and "General Taylor Never Surrenders." Reverse: grape vines and tendrils with legend, "A little more grape, Captain Bragg." Dark amber. Attributed to Baltimore Glass Works. H. 6⅛ in. Mattatuck

"Old Rough and Ready," Zachary Taylor, was another military hero who appealed to the masses. He was a hero of the Indian Wars and led troops to victory in the war with Mexico. The slogan, "A Little More Grape, Captain Bragg," appears on the reverse of one Taylor flask and refers to the legend that Taylor, upon learning in the field that he was going to be asked to run for President said to his informant, "Have a little more grape, Captain Bragg." Obviously, such a self-effacing man who was already a national hero and a drinker, besides, would help sell more whiskey and more bottles.

A gauge of Taylor's popularity when he ran for office in 1849 is the number of flasks made with his picture or legends portraying his career as a soldier. There are close to thirty known Taylor flasks with various subjects on the reverse sides. There are many on which Taylor shares the limelight with George Washington.

It might be interesting to consider that the above-mentioned flasks—with the exception of Washington and Adams—commemorate presidents who were not known

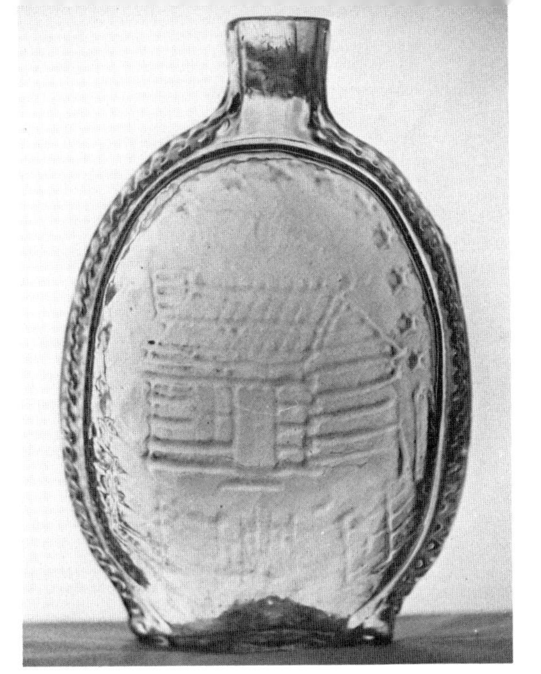

for their temperance. Whiskey flasks are a fitting monument to Andrew Jackson, William Henry Harrison, and Zachary Taylor, all of whom were known to be hard-fighting and hard-drinking men. Their natural appeal to the moldmakers and especially to the glassblowers who, because of their relatively high pay and short hours were also known for their heavy drinking habits, might be one reason why so many flasks were made which portrayed these men. Most particularly, it was the customer who bought the booze to whom these heroes appealed. The glassmakers were happy to give the customer what he wanted.

Flask of the Harrison campaign showing log cabin on obverse and American flag flying over cider barrel on reverse side. Over the barrel in semi-circle is "Hard Cider." Pale aqua. Mattatuck

Lafayette flask in dark amber is initialled "T. S." for Thomas Stebbins of the Coventry, Connecticut, Glass Works. The reverse is Masonic emblems. H. $7\frac{3}{8}$ *in.* Mattatuck

Profile of Lafayette facing right on obverse with name of glass house misspelled. Dark amber. Reverse: French Liberty Cap on pole. "S & S" stands for Stebbins and Stebbins. H. $7\frac{3}{8}$ *in.* Mattatuck

Chapter 7

COMMEMORATIVE HISTORICAL FLASKS

TWO nineteenth-century visitors to America were commemorated on whiskey flasks. A great many flasks with a variety of motifs were made to celebrate the return of General Lafayette to this country in August, 1824. A national celebration lasted over a year, with Lafayette going back to his native France in September, 1825. Glass flasks were but one of the variety of souvenirs made during this period. Women wore Lafayette buckles on their shoes and men wore vests embroidered or printed with the hero's likeness. People ate off plates that celebrated Lafayette's coming and drank from teacups that bore prints of his face.

While in America, Lafayette visited every state in the country and was feted by Masonic lodges in every town. As Lafayette and his party visited each town, they were greeted with a great deal of celebration and ceremony. Speeches, banquets, fireworks, and processions marked similar events throughout the country and there is no question that much whiskey and rum was consumed in honor of the French hero. Commemorative flasks were a

This Lafayette flask in dark yellow-green was made at the Mount Vernon Glass Works. Masonic motifs on reverse. H. 7¼ in. Mattatuck

fitting tribute of a country gone wild in welcoming the Revolutionary War hero.

It was left to the Staffordshire potters to romanticize Lafayette's triumphant return to these shores. Scenes of the Frenchman visiting the tombs of Benjamin Franklin and George Washington were common motifs for plates and jugs. The glassblowers of America were not to be sobered by these events and commemorated, instead, only the happy fact of Lafayette's presence as a cause for celebration. The fact that the visit was a long one that encompassed the entire nation was fortuitous for the bottle makers. It gave them time to make and market a large quantity of Lafayette and Masonic flasks. There is little doubt that Lafayette flasks were popular long after the hero had departed these shores for the last time.

An interesting flask commemorating Lafayette's visit was made in Coventry, Connecticut, and three variations of the same flask have been found. These are the DeWitt Clinton flasks, and it is doubtful that Clinton would have been commemorated in glass at all had Lafayette not been there to share the honors with him when "Clinton's Ditch," the Erie Canal, was opened. Although the official opening of the Canal did not take place until a month after Lafayette's departure, the Frenchman did find time during his visit to stop off and view Clinton's great accomplishment.

Lafayette's profile, facing right, is within Masonic arch on this flask made by Knox and McKee in Wheeling, (West) Virginia. Color clear. Eagle on reverse. Note "N" is backwards on this flask also.
Mattatuck

Almost all the remainder of the Lafayette flasks have Masonic motifs on the reverse sides, although there is one flask made at the Kensington Glass Works that has an eagle on the reverse and the initials of Dr. Dyott in a panel under the eagle. Some of the flasks made in Coventry, Connecticut, have the initials of Thomas Stebbins, the maker, on them.

Another visitor to this country who found herself the subject of portrait flasks when she arrived was Jenny Lind. P. T. Barnum, the great entrepreneur, brought the "Swedish Nightingale" to this country in 1850. America welcomed her with open arms as a result of the six months of intense advance publicity that had saturated the nation before her arrival.

ABOVE: *Lafayette shares this flask, made at Coventry, Connecticut, with DeWitt Clinton. Initialled "T. S." for Thomas Stebbins. "C-T" is abbreviation used for Connecticut. Dark olive-green. H. 5⅞ in.* Mattatuck

RIGHT: *DeWitt Clinton appears on another Lafayette flask, also made at Coventry. H. 6 in.* Mattatuck

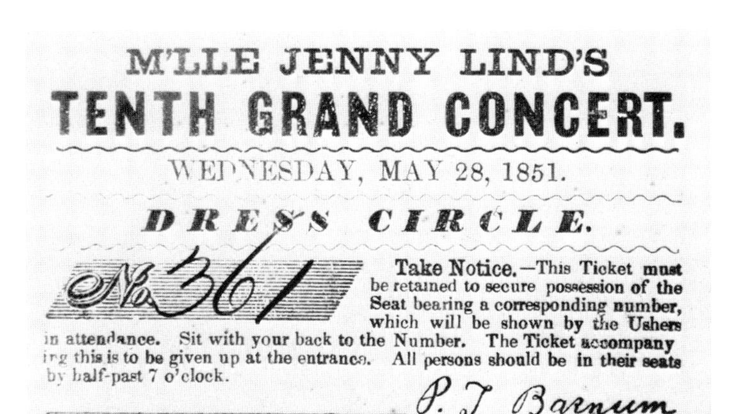
M'LLE JENNY LIND'S

TENTH GRAND CONCERT.

WEDNESDAY, MAY 28, 1851.

DRESS CIRCLE.

No 361

Take Notice.—This Ticket must be retained to secure possession of the Seat bearing a corresponding number, which will be shown by the Ushers in attendance. Sit with your back to the Number. The Ticket accompanying this is to be given up at the entrance. All persons should be in their seats by half-past 7 o'clock.

Van Norden & Amerman, Printers, 60 William-st.

P. T. Barnum

BELOW LEFT: *Jenny Lind, the "Swedish Nightingale," is shown in three-quarters view facing left, wearing large Bertha collar for which she was known. Flask is aqua and the same on both sides. H 7 in.* Mattatuck

RIGHT: *Jenny Lind flask with branches running up sides. Light aqua. H. 8¾ in.* Mattatuck

ABOVE: *Ticket to Jenny Lind concert signed by P. T. Barnum, 1851.* Mattatuck

Miss Lind, the only woman to have been immortalized on American glass flasks, appears on at least twelve different bottles, most of which are in the *calabash* shape. The portrait, always the same view, was copied from the only available likeness that Barnum had of the singer before her arrival. This one picture was used widely on posters, broadsides, and advertisements. There is less detail than is found in most of the flask portraits, probably because no one knew exactly what she looked like. The familiar outline of the three-quarter bust turned to the left and the wide bertha collar became a symbolic picture of the singer. Besides the calabash Jenny Lind bottles, there are several scroll flasks with the singer's likeness embossed over a lyre.

Jenny Lind calabash bottle showing house on reverse side. Light aqua. H. 8¾ in. Mattatuck

The growth of American industry following the War of 1812 became the subject of some glass whiskey flasks. A great many "Success to the Railroad" flasks were made to commemorate various rail lines being opened. The early railroads are shown with the first horse-drawn cars embossed on the flasks. Later flasks, made around 1850, show steam locomotives.

Political slogans were used as decoration on flasks, also. "The American System," a slogan coined by Henry Clay, signifies the approval of protective tariffs to allow national industries to grow with a minimum of outside competition. This slogan also embraced the Federal development of methods of transportation such as waterways and road improvements. The reverse of "The American System" flask is an embossed riverboat.

"Liberty and Union" and "Corn For The World" were two other slogans familiar enough to have been placed on flasks. The latter celebrated the repeal of the English Corn Laws in 1846.

Another event of national importance that was the subject of a great many of the later embossed flasks was the 1859 gold rush which resulted from the rumor of gold being discovered in Colorado. The crowds of hopeful prospectors were called "Pike's Peakers" and the flasks commemorating this were probably the last large

Flask showing paddlewheel steamboat flying American flag. Legend: "The American System." Reverse: sheaf of wheat and legend: "Use me but do not abuse me." Made by Bakewell, Pace and Bakewell, Pittsburgh. Dark olive-green. Mattatuck

ABOVE: *"Railroad" flask Obverse: horse drawing cart on rails "Lowell Railroad." Reverse: American eagle. Made in Coventry, Connecticut, Pint. Olive-green.* Mattatuck

RIGHT: *"Success to the Railroad flask in medium blue shows locomotive on rails. Reverse is the same. H. 6¾ in.* Mattatuck

"Corn for the world" flask made by the Baltimore Glass Works. Olive-green. H. 6½ in. Mattatuck

Early Masonic flask in dark amber was made at Coventry Glass Works. Note the large "G" on reverse side is reversed. H. 6 in. Mattatuck

group of pictorial flasks made in the nineteenth century.

Throughout the history of flask manufacture in America the most popular symbol used was the American eagle. Adopted as a symbol of the new republic in 1782, the eagle is found on more flasks than any other single motif. He is depicted in a large variety of poses and on the earliest flasks he is his most vigorous. As designs for flasks, eagles were freely adapted from contemporary coins. On many flasks the eagle is on the reverse as well as the obverse sides, and on some he is used on the opposite side in conjunction with portraits or Masonic motifs.

Another symbol of the free republic used less frequently than the eagle is the bust of Columbia which was probably also adapted from contemporary coins. The American flag was used on several flasks and perhaps one of the reasons it was used less often than other national motifs was that it is not a satisfying design for embossment on a glass bottle. Since it is an asymmetrical object it is not particularly appealing in line outline without the use of colors.

A great number of Masonic flasks were made and, as was noted in a previous chapter, many were commemorative of Lafayette's visit to America. However, the brotherhood was extremely popular in the early part of the nineteenth century. Flasks with Masonic symbols such as the pavement, pillars, keys, compass, etc., were made in abundance by many glassmakers. In 1830 a scandal arose surrounding the Masonic organization that ended the manufacture of flasks with its representative symbols.

A renegade Mason of New York State, whose efforts to establish a new chapter of the fraternity in Batavia, New York, had been thwarted because members of his original chapter in LeRoy did not want him listed as a

OPPOSITE PAGE
TOP: *Masonic flask made by White Glass Works, Zanesville, Ohio. J. Shepard & Co. Note "S" in Shepard is backwards. Dark amber. H. 6¾ in.* Mattatuck

BOTTOM: *Flask with Masonic emblems is dark olive-green and is the same on both sides. Attributed to Coventry, Connecticut. H. 6 in.* Mattatuck

LEFT: *Concentric ring eagle flask is the same on both sides. Clear, very heavy light aqua glass. Attributed to Keene, New Hampshire. H. 7⅛ in.* Mattatuck

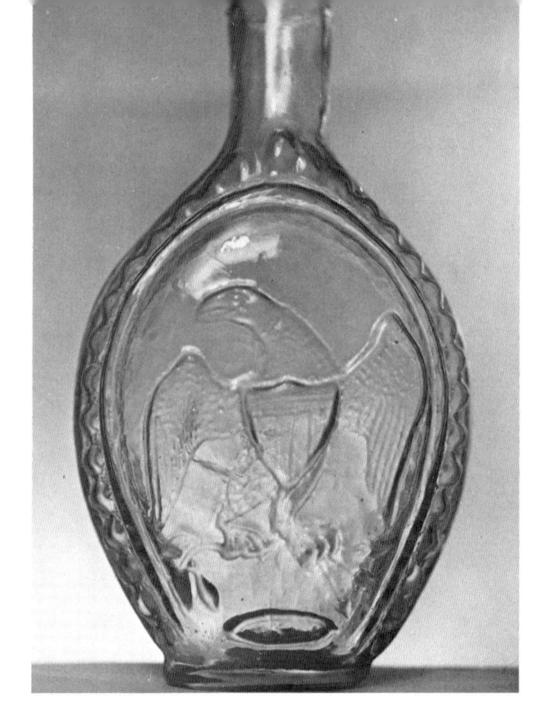

This eagle flask is light yellow-green and was made in the Monongahela-Pittsburgh area. H. 6¾ in. Mattatuck

One of only a couple of known flasks using the flag as decoration. Pint size in olive amber glass. Shape dates it to c. 1860. Mattatuck

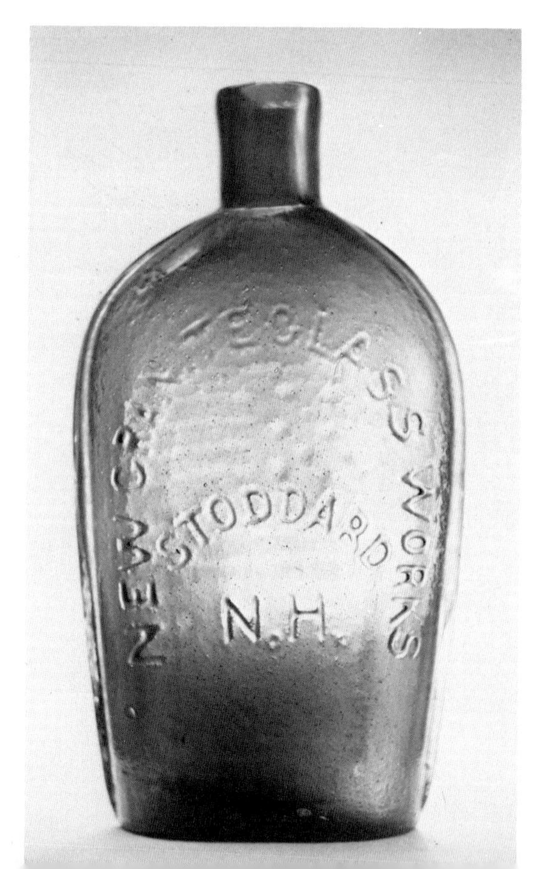

charter member, threatened to write a book divulging the secrets of the Masonic Order. This would-be author, William Morgan, was kidnapped and was never heard from again. Events following this disappearance led to strong public sentiment against secret organizations in a democratic society and an anti-Masonry political party was formed.

This movement grew from the organization of small local bands of the Batavia area until it encompassed the central government of New York State and eventually spread throughout the country. The movement lasted until the mid-1840s. Although large rewards were offered for information concerning Mr. Morgan's disappearance, he was never found. American glassmakers had long before stopped using the motifs of the Masonic brotherhood on their flasks.

LEFT: *Large flask with elliptical sunburst motif. Attributed to Keene, New Hampshire, Glass House or possibly, Mount Vernon. Heavy clear pale green glass. H. 7¾ in.* Mattatuck RIGHT: *"Violin" or "scroll" flask. Cornflower blue. H. 6¾ in.* Mattatuck

LEFT: *Pale blue "violin" or "scroll" flask. H. 8¾ in.* Mattatuck RIGHT: *Early flask with bull's eye and "Jared Spencer." Reverse: same, but with "Manchester, Conn." H. 6 in.* Mattatuck

Chapter 8

PICTORIAL FLASKS

PICTORIAL flasks were made before the flasks with historical motifs and slogans and continued to be made for a short while after the historical flasks lost their popularity. Pictorial flasks have no particular historical significance, but the various images on their surfaces are usually motifs that are decorative and contemporary.

The sunburst was a common motif for the earliest embossed flasks. The symmetrical design was easily adaptable to the early flask shape. Several sunburst flask designs were made at Keene, New Hampshire; Coventry, Connecticut; and Mount Vernon, New York.

The cornucopia was embossed on many flasks, and the motif was used through a rather long period. On several of this type of flask the horn-of-plenty is depicted upside-down and the bounty is spilling out. On others it is in the upright position. It is probable that this symbol of fertility and plenty appealed to the nineteenth-century farmers of America.

Although pictorial flasks were made for a longer period, it is obvious that the historical flasks were more

TOP PAIR: *Early flask with eagle and cornucopia. Possibly made at Pitkin Glass Works in Connecticut. Dark olive-green. H. 6 in. c. 1810.*
Mattatuck

BOTTOM PAIR: *Marked cornucopia and eagle flask (early) in dark green glass. "J. P. F." under eagle are initials of J. P. Foster of Manchester Glass Works (Pitkin) after 1810. "Conn." under eagle on reverse. H. 6 in.* Mattatuck

popular. There are far fewer pictorial flasks than historical. A great many of the existing pictorial flasks are rather late. Around 1850 the glassmakers began producing flasks with clasped hands and double eagles embossed. The eagles no longer look as belligerent as they did on earlier flasks.

There is one interesting pictorial flask that has a tree embossed on either side. Both trees look identical, but if one looks carefully, a small bird can be seen perched on a limb of one of the trees. Another flask commemorates a popular song, "Not For Joe," while yet another has classical profiles in relief on either side that are thought to be Byron and Scott.

On one pictorial flask there is a scene of two men sitting at a tavern table, the other side a caricature of a man as yet to be identified. A ballet dancer adorns a flask made by Chapmen of Baltimore, Maryland. The reverse is a soldier carrying a gun.

A group of flasks were made that have come to be known as the "scroll" or "violin" flasks because of their

Flask with cornucopia and urn of fruit. Dark aqua. Same flask was made at several different glass houses, two of which were Keene and Coventry H. 5¼ in. Mattatuck

"Scott" and "Byron" flask. Dark green H. 5½ in.
Mattatuck

shape. There were quite a few versions of this, which is an interesting shape and almost qualifies for being a figural, rather than a pictorial, bottle.

In general, the early sunburst flasks are typical of the first flask shape made in America. These had wide shoulders and sides that tapered downwards. Later flasks became rounder, leaving a more suitable flat surface for embossments. They were made in two-piece molds that were hinged on the bottom. As the historical flasks went out of favor, whiskey flasks began to look more like bottles and a great many carried embossments of the glassworks where they had been made on one side and a picture or decoration on the other.

With the simplified shape came embossments that were somewhat simplified as well. Flasks with long necks and bulbous bodies were made for the Jenny Lind flasks. These bottles are called "calabash." The scroll flasks are interesting because the decoration in the embossing was so suited to the shape of the bottle.

One interesting late bottle that is scarce today is the

"Apostle" bottle. This whiskey bottle has a broad round base and a long neck. Embossed around the bottle, from the base to about halfway up, are six Gothic arches, each with a monk enclosed. This design was adapted from a Staffordshire pottery pitcher made in the 1830s, evidently to please the Catholic clergy. Since this type of bottle is scarce, it is obvious that the Church could not condone the apostles as decoration for a whiskey container.

A bottle that is in great demand today by collectors is the "Great Western." This bottle features an embossment of a full-faced figure of a pioneer in buckskin suit and broad-brimmed hat and a belt with a knife stuck in it. Embossed above the figure, which has a rifle in the left hand, is "The Great Western." On the reverse is a buck with large antlers, facing to the left. Three other flasks feature embossments of hunters.

Sheaves of rye and wheat or bunches of grapes are also used to decorate pictorial flasks. The morning glory has been employed as the motif on at least one flask, but oddly enough, flowers as motifs were not common. Many

Flask advertising glass works. Profile of man unidentified. Light aqua. Reverse: "Fair View Works" and view of house. H. 6 in. Mattatuck

Light aqua flask made by Coffin and Hay, Hammonton, New Jersey. Obverse: eagle with shield. Reverse: bunch of grapes. H. 7⅛ in. Mattatuck.

"Tree" flask, sapphire blue in quart size. Both sides appear similar, but there is a difference. On obverse the tree is in full foliage, but there are many large buds. On reverse, the buds are gone and a bird is perched on limb on left branch. Mattatuck

"Pike's Peak" flask in light aqua shows traveler on obverse with pick and bundle over shoulder. Reverse has peaceful eagle seen only on later flasks. H. 7½ in. Mattatuck

Flask shapes changed toward middle of century. Obverse shows ballet dancer and "Chapmen" (Glass Works). The reverse side has a soldier and "Balt. Md.". Pint size. Light aqua. c. 1860. Mattatuck

"Jester" flask shows stout man with cane behind back and wearing high hat, jesting with another man in long tailcoat and umbrella. Reverse shows full-faced man with arm under his chin. Dark blue. H. 6⅜ in. Mattatuck

of the pictorial flasks were made rather late and have little embossment except the name of the glassworks where they were made, a depression for a paper label from the distillers or bottlers, and possibly a small embossment such as a few stars.

There is a wide choice of both historical and pictorial flasks for the determined collector. Once available in abundance, these flasks have been collected longer than any other American bottles, and museums have long recognized their value. Since historical and pictorial flasks have all of the best qualities—age, beauty, and, for some, rarity—for collectible items, they are an excellent investment. The wary collector, however, should know the characteristics of old American glass before he invests heavily in the early flasks. There have been copies made of some of them and while many of the copies, themselves, have value, it is best for the collector to approach the market armed with sufficient knowledge to tell the real from the reproduction.

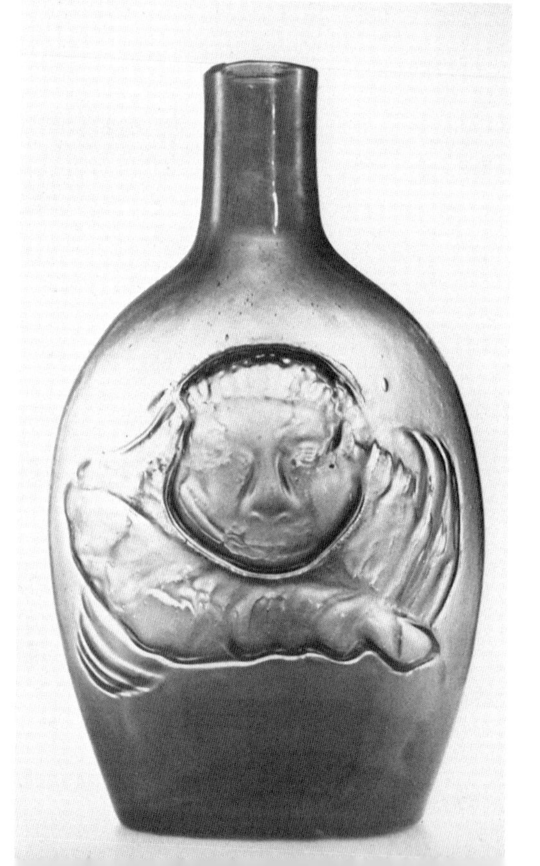

Chapter 9

WINE AND GIN BOTTLES

WINE is one of the oldest intoxicating beverages known to mankind. Fermented grape juice was probably consumed by prehistoric man. Grape juice ferments naturally and ordinary wine is, therefore, less complicated to make than other beverages with alcoholic content. Wine making began in the Near East which was the natural home of the European grape. Introduced by the ancient Greeks to Europe and spread by the Romans throughout the Empire, wine was used as a table drink, a health aid, and in religious ceremonies throughout the history of civilized mankind.

The Spaniards were the first to introduce wine making to America and the missionaries in California were the first to produce it. In 1820 Joseph Chapman planted the first vineyard in California in the area of Los Angeles. Chapman started what has become one of the most important industries in that state.

Wine bottles were the first bottles to be imported to this country. Those early bottles were free-blown by British glassmakers and were, for the most part similar,

Bottling and corking.

Fine clear weather is best for bottling all sorts of wines, and much cleanliness is required. The first consideration, in bottling wines, is to examine and see if the wines are in a proper state. *The wines should be fine and brilliant*, or they will never brighten after.

The bottles must be all sound, clean and dry, with plenty of good sound corks.

The cork is to be put in with the hand, and then driven well in with a flat wooden mallet, the weight of which ought to be a *pound and a quarter*, but however, not to exceed a pound and a half, for if the mallet be too light or too heavy it will not drive the cork in *properly*, and may *break the bottle*. The corks must so completely fill up the neck of each bottle as to render them *air tight*, but leave a space of an inch between the wine and the cork.

When all the wine is bottled, it is to be stored in a cool cellar, and *on no account on the bottles' bottoms*, but on their sides and in saw-dust.

Apparatus for wine making.

To make wine well, and with facility, persons should have all the requisite apparatus, namely, the vats, vat-staff, fruit-bruiser, strainer, hair-bags, wine-press, thermometer, and bottling machine.

Mr Carnell's receipt for red gooseberry wine.

Take cold soft water, 10 gallons,—red gooseberries, 11 gallons, and ferment. Now mix raw sugar, 16 lbs.—beet-root, sliced, 2 lbs. and red tartar, in fine powder, 3 ounces. Afterwards put in sassafras chips, 1 lb. and brandy, 1 gallon, or

Directions for bottling home-made wine from 1825 "receipt" book. Watkins

LEFT: *Demijohn. Black glass with open pontil, laid on ring on neck. H. 18 in. c. 1820.* Author

BELOW: *Wine tester was dropped down into barrels. Made by Lake Dunmore Glass Works, Middlebury, Vermont. Pontil mark. Light aqua. 1833-43.* Mattatuck

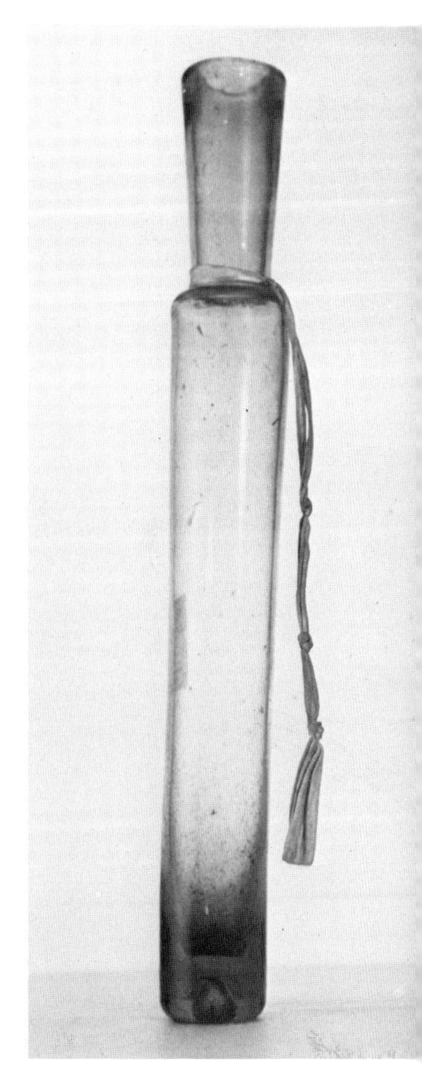

if not the same, in shape. Dutch bottles, resembling the English bottles, were also sent here during the eighteenth century. The free-blown bottles differ in that the necks of the British bottles are usually longer than the Dutch. The Dutch bottles have a large kick-up or pushed-up hump in the base. These bottles are all bulbous and squat and are called "squat" bottles or "onion" bottles.

Early wine bottles held in high esteem are those with wafer-shaped seals applied to them in which was impressed the name of a tavern keeper, a distiller or a patron. Since aging is important to the quality of wine, these seals often bear a date. When the date places the bottle in the seventeenth century, it becomes most desirable to collectors in England as well as in this country. When the seal can be identified as being that of an historic personage the bottle's value is further enhanced.

A type of wine bottle wanted by collectors is the large bulk bottle that holds as much as ten gallons. These, called demijohns, are also free-blown, usually of dark green or black glass which shows many impurities, Demi-

RIGHT: *Wine or spirits bottle. Black glass. Double-collared lip. Late nineteenth century.*
Rebner

BELOW: *Blown wine bottle, deep kick-up bottom, pontilled. Pale aqua, many bubbles, whittle marked. Laid-on ring neck. H. 11¾ in.*
Rebner

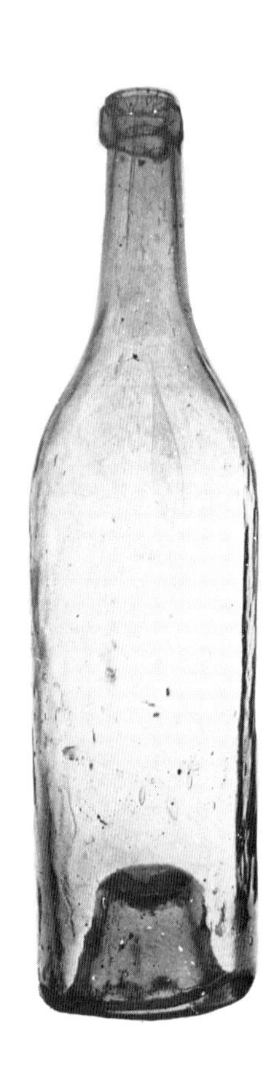

johns were used to transport other liquids besides wine, but they are generally placed in this category.

In the same general category as the demijohn is the carboy, a later bottle of cylindrical shape. Also made of cheap glass in colors similar to demijohns, these bottles were made in various sizes. The bulk bottles were usually covered in wicker to prevent breakage in transport. It was not uncommon for the early glass houses to have a wicker room on the premises where apprentices and women were put to work weaving these covers.

Nineteenth-century wine bottles are usually cylindrical and this shape is most commonly used today. During the late 1800s a method of polishing cylindrical bottles by turning them in the mold while they were being blown was devised. No seam mark shows on bottles finished in this manner and they have a highly polished surface. Although with the development of the plate mold it became customary to emboss many bottles, wine bottles are almost always plain, and labels are used for identification.

Since nineteenth-century wine bottles offer little variety for the collector, they have been somewhat neglected. Carboys, seal bottles, and demijohns have long been in demand, but most often in conjunction with general collections of old mouth-blown bottles. Because wine making is one of the oldest Californian industries, if not the oldest, an interesting collection in that state might include the various bottles that have been used by the industry. A collateral collection of the printed labels and advertising that represents California wine production would be interesting to gather also.

Gin, a strong liquor consisting of grain alcohol and juniper berries or other flavoring, was originally sold as a medicine in England. Gin was first discovered in Holland in the middle of the seventeenth century and al-

WINES AND LIQUORS.

WE GO FOR THE UNION.
DR. UNDERHILL'S PURE UNION WINE,
ISABELLA CATAWBA,
From CROTON POINT, of excellent quality.
FOR SALE AT HIS
PURE WINE AND GRAPE DEPOT,
No. 7 Clinton Hall, Astor-place.

HORSES AND CARRIAGES.

Wine merchant's advertisement from New York Times, *April 16, 1861.* Mattatuck

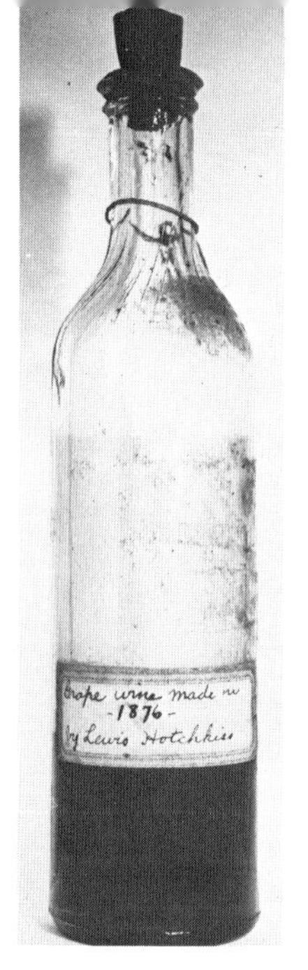

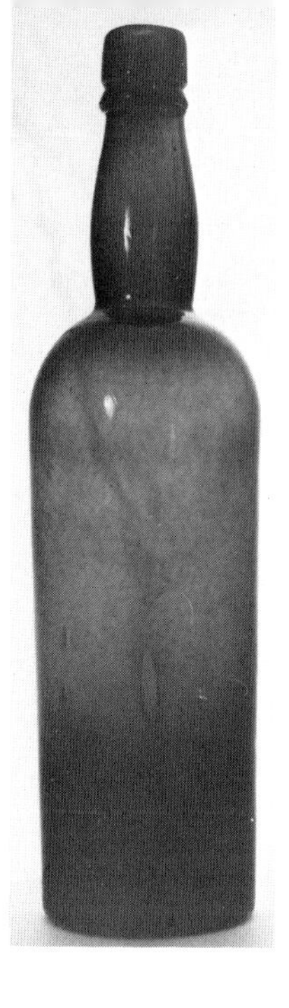

LEFT: *"Grape wine made in 1876 by Lewis Hotchkiss," (Connecticut). Note stretch marks on neck of old bottle. H. 9¼ in.* Rebner

CENTER: *Turn-mold wine bottle with graphite pontil in dark olive-green was dug in Maine woods. H. 12 in.* Curulla

RIGHT: *Automatic bottle machine bottle has embossment of post-Prohibition bottles. H. 12 in.* Author

though dispensed as a medicine in the beginning, it soon became a popular drink in Holland and England. Due to its low cost and high alcoholic content, the "medicine" appealed to the masses and apothecaries soon went into the business of distilling it. The drink was consumed in enormous amounts until King George II placed a high tax on the beverage in order to sober up his subjects.

Apothecaries once more went back to selling gin as a medicine (which was not taxed) and disguised the drink by adding bitters flavoring. This was, of course, the beginning of the great bitters and patent medicine era which lasted throughout the nineteenth century.

The earliest gin bottles used were indistinguishable from other types of bottles, primarily demijohns, used for transporting liquids. The one type of bottle of a distinguished shape that was used mainly for gin, but for other purposes as well, is the case bottle. This is a square tapered bottle of amber, green or black glass. These bottles were made in Holland, England, and America. The earliest case bottles were blown and shaped, probably with the aid of a trowel or paddle. Early case bottles will, of course, have pontil scars on the bases and sheared necks.

The case bottle was made and used for gin in the nineteenth century and those with embossments may safely be placed in the latter part of that century. Case bottles were made in a variety of sizes ranging from a half-pint to several gallons. The obvious advantage of this distinctive shape is that it was safer and more economical to pack for shipping than the amorphous demijohn.

As is true of early wine bottles, there are few collectors who specialize only in case gin bottles. Often collectors want one or two early examples if they are making comprehensive collections of early glass. The late nineteenth-century case bottles, however, with their distinctive embossments, are always desired by collectors.

LEFT: *"Ludlow" or "chestnut" bottle. Applied lip, kick-up base and pontil mark. Light aqua. H. 9 in.* Rebner

RIGHT: *Interesting case gin bottle has shingle effect on surface and nail marks down sides. H. 10½ in.* Rebner

DISTILLATION.

The object of distillation is the preparation of alcohol or pure spirit, which is obtained from brandy, rum, arrack, and whiskey, prepared from wine, sugar, rice, and malt. It also includes compound spirits, or those which, in addition to alcohol, contain some volatile or pungent oil or essence,—as gin, hollands, caraway, and peppermint; the essential oils, as oil of cinnamon, oil of cloves, oil of peppermint, and otto of roses; and the simple distilled waters, which retain the fragrant flavour of the particular herbs with which they have been distilled.

To manage distillation.

Previous to distilling, the processes of brewing and fermentation are necessary. In distilling, there is only one general rule, namely, to let the heat, in all cases, be as gentle as possible. A water-bath, if sufficiently large, is preferable to any other mode, and will perform the operation with all the dispatch requisite for the most extensive business. The spirit, as it first comes over, should be received into a quantity of cold water; as, by this means, the connexion between it and the oily matter will be considerably lessened. For the same reason, after it has been once rectified in the water-bath, it should be again mixed with an equal quantity of

By laying the hand on the still and capital, as the fire gains strength, the process of the operation will be ascertained; for, whenever the head, or capital, feels hot, it is a proof that the volatile particles have arisen, and are about to enter the worm. When the still head is about to become hot, prepare a *damp*, made of the ashes under the grate, mixed with as much water as will properly wet them. This mixture is to be thrown upon the fire, to moderate its action, at the instant when distillation has commenced. Continue the heat as long as the distilled liquid is spirituous to the taste. When the distilled liquor carries with it any particular flavour, it should be re-distilled with essential oils, in order to convert it into a compound spirit, as gin, peppermint, and other cordials.

When all the spirituous fluid is drawn off, the still should be emptied by a cock in the side. The head, &c. should then be removed, and the several lutes taken clean off. The still may now be charged a second time, and luted. If the spirit, or compound to be made, is of a different nature or flavour from that procured by the last distillation, the still, capital, and worm should be thoroughly cleaned by hot water, sand, and a scrubbing brush, to remove the oily particles which adhere to their internal surfaces. The worm is best cleansed by

ABOVE: *How to make home-made whiskey. From book published in 1825.* Watkins

RIGHT: *Dark brown "chestnut" flask. Banded neck, pontil mark, kick-up base. H. 7 in. c. 1800.* Mattatuck

Chapter 10

COLLECTIBLE WHISKEY BOTTLES

COLLECTORS from the eastern part of the United States, especially those who have been collecting for long enough to have acquired some of the early pictorial and historical flasks, often lose sight of the fact that many of these whiskey flasks were made before the West was settled. Bottles made before 1840 are, therefore, of little regional interest to the Westerner. In the West the bottles of local whiskey companies of the middle of the nineteenth century and later are often in more demand than the earlier flasks of the New England region. Interest in these later whiskey bottles has spread across the country.

The history of the settling of the West is closely tied with the history of the whiskey business in the same area. The gold rush of 1849 brought thousands of settlers as far as the coast and necessitated the shipping of goods to this area. Provisions were brought into San Francisco harbor, and not the least of these was whiskey. Very many whiskey distributors went in and out of business,

LEFT: *Whiskey flask, dark amber, applied handle and pontil scar. H. 8 in. c. 1850.* Hardy

RIGHT: *Whisky flask, ¾ quart size. Dark brown. Raised round medallion "Chestnut Grove Whiskey/C. W." Crown motif in center. Reverse has sunken panel for label. c. 1860.* Mattatuck

LEFT: *Booz bottle in shape of house. Chamfered roof. Dark amber. Although bearing date "1840" on back roof, this bottle is thought to have been made at a somewhat later date in the nineteenth century. H. 7¾ in.* Mattatuck

RIGHT: *Early reproduction of Booz bottle which has been reproduced many times since. Note roof on this bottle is not chamfered and there are two dots under the "t" in "St." Also, there are dotted tracings across surface of bottle. Yellow-green. H. 7¾ in. c. 1865.* Mattatuck

thereby supplying a large variety of bottles for today's collector.

While the majority of the early bottles that are collected by Western bottle collectors were made by Eastern glass houses, many were made to order for the Western bottlers and distillers. These bottles with embossing that have the names and addresses of various Pacific Coast distributors are of prime interest to those collectors who are interested in the historical and geographical facts concerning regional industries. Prices paid for the rare bottles of this type often exceed the current prices of the earlier historical flasks.

There are several reasons for the popularity of whiskey bottles of the latter half of the nineteenth century in the West. First of all, since the history of the settling of the West is so short in comparison with the history of Eastern United States, there are few artifacts from which to choose in the way of regional collectible items. While it took a hundred years for New Englanders to consider the early flasks historically important and of enough in-

Three whiskey flasks. Flask in center has double applied collar and strap sides and is called "shoo-fly" or coffin flask. Flask on right is "pumpkin seed" shape. "Warranted Flask" on left; h. 6¼ in. c. 1890. Rebner

terest and beauty to be worth collecting, collectors in the Californian area seem to have a more immediate sense of the history of their region.

There are few true "antiques" of the old West. In recent years there have been so many objects shipped from the East to the West coast by antique dealers who are beginning to realize that the truly desirable items in that part of the country are those that were brought out and used by the early settlers. Therefore, many nineteenth-century items that are not collected in the East have more meaning to the Californian. Western whiskey bottles are one of the few articles that truly represent the history of the area in which they are found.

Beside the regional historical interest in whiskey bottles with embossments, glass bottles made before 1900 were blown in the mold and have the added quality of having been made by hand. This is not true of many other collectible items of the late nineteenth century.

One other aspect of bottle collecting for the Westerner that has led to a phenomenon second only to the original

ABOVE: *Whiskey or spirits bottle with large bull's eye design. Dark green, applied double collar. H. 8¾ in.* Mattatuck

RIGHT: *Three pre-Prohibition embossed whiskey flasks. c. 1890.* Rebner

LEFT: *Golden amber "shoo-fly" whiskey flask with strap sides. "S" embossed on base. H. 7½ in.* Rebner

RIGHT: *Amber "T" flask. Collectors look for embossments on these later flasks. H. 8¼ in.* Rebner

gold rush, is that the bottles are available for the seeking. Digging for bottles in the desert has definite advantages over digging in the variable climate of New England. While the yield may be the same for a bottle digger who happens onto a "good dump" in New England, the days are not as numerous when he can dig, nor are the dumps as easy to find. Abandoned towns of the old West are being repopulated on weekends by campers who search for bottles and other artifacts that might be of historical interest.

The enthusiasm for regional artifacts in the West has led to the growth of many clubs for bottle collectors. Collectors gather to pool information concerning their latest finds and to sell and trade bottles. A great deal of the literature on old glass bottles has come from Western writers and collectors. Information about whiskey bottles is limited to the period between 1850 and 1920, which was the start of national Prohibition. Because this has become the period of bottle manufacture about which the most information has been disseminated,

whiskey bottles of this period are in high demand, not only in the West, but among bottle collectors everywhere.

In this category of bottle collecting, age alone is not a criterion for value. Those whiskey bottles that command high prices in the West are those attributed to distillers or bottlers whose bottles are rarely found. The bottles themselves are similar in size and shape, but are in demand if the name of the bottler and the California address are embossed. An unmarked bottle can be of little value, whereas an identical embossed bottle may bring a very high price. Similar regional bottles bearing the names and addresses of Eastern bottlers are of little importance to the collector as yet.

Whiskey bottles are somewhat easier to date than bottles in other categories. The earliest whiskey bottles were, of course, the pictorial and historical flasks. The embossed whiskey bottles were made later in the nineteenth century and the fact that Prohibition began in 1920 and lasted until 1933 provides an interesting cut-off date for

ABOVE: *Narrow pocket flask in clear glass. "¼ pt." embossed on bottom. Early automatic bottle machine bottle.*
Curulla

RIGHT: *Whiskey bottles from 1 quart to ¼ pint. c. 1885-1910.* Rebner

LEFT: *Three miniature whiskey flasks. Center flask is copy of early Keene whiskey flask. Flask on right, earlier than others, has ribs halfway and zinc screw cap; sun-tinted amethyst. H. (flask on right) 6¼ in.* Rebner

embossed whiskey bottles that were made in quantity. From 1933 until 1964 all whiskey bottles had to be marked with the sentence, "FEDERAL LAW FORBIDS SALE OR REUSE OF THIS BOTTLE." Naturally, all the other criteria for dating bottles may be applied to whiskey bottles in order to identify further the method and time of manufacture.

One of the most unique and interesting of all whiskey bottles of the latter half of the nineteenth century is the Booz bottle in the shape of a log-cabin. This bottle, although dated 1840, was made around 1860 and has been reproduced several times since. The early reproductions are scarce and expensive now. An original Booz bottle is almost impossible to find.

Collecting old whiskey bottles offers a wide variety of embossments, but a smaller variety of shapes and colors. Clear glass is most often used but green and amber glass are not uncommon. Blue whiskey bottles are rare and command high prices.

Whiskey flasks made during Prohibition are interesting

BELOW: *Johann Hoff malt liquor bottle. Amber (this bottle usually found in olive-green). c. 1890.* Rebner

for collectors. Many of these flasks in which whiskey was sold "for medicinal purposes" had shot-glass closures. Another category of whiskey bottles is that of the miniatures still being made. The older ones are very much in demand.

The whiskey bottle collector can also interest himself in collateral material such as advertising trays, glasses, trade cards, newspaper advertisements, and articles and posters concerning Prohibition. Advertising items for bars are also collected.

Ladies' pocket flasks were popular when whiskey was illegal. Left, silver overlay on glass. Right, pattern glass, silver cap. H. 4 in. Hardy

Chapter 11

BLOWN THREE-MOLD DECANTERS AND BOTTLES

OBVIOUSLY, a great many of the bottles that have been made by American glass houses were containers for liquor. Along with free-blown pocket flasks, decanters for the table were also made by the same method. English and Irish glass decanters were imported, also. The American glass houses could not compete in the field of decorative glass until 1820, when a type of glass making was devised that would turn out clear patterned glass table decanters that could compare with English or Irish blown glass both in attractiveness and price.

The blown three-mold decanter was the major article made by this method of shaping glass. Elaborate patterns could be achieved with little or no handwork by the use of hinged molds. Many of the patterns used were copied from the more expensive English or Irish prototypes.

Patterned blown three-mold glass can be distinguished from cut or pressed glass easily, since the inner surface of the glass will be concave where the corresponding outer surface is convex and vice versa. As many as 140

LEFT: *Blown-in-mold decanter in dark green glass. Attributed to Keene, New Hampshire Glass Works. Early nineteenth century. H. 7⅛ in.* Mattatuck

RIGHT: *Blown-three-mold decanter in baroque pattern. Matching blown stopper. H. 8½ in.* Mattatuck

different patterns for this type of glass have been recorded and often one decanter will have a combination of several patterns. Shapes as well as patterns were fashioned after the British cut-glass decanters. Considering the short time—only twenty years—that blown three-mold decanters were made, there is a large variety available to the collector. One can only surmise that these decanters were extremely popular.

The majority was made in clear flint glass. A decanter in any other color is considered rare. One feature of the round decanters is that many of them have laid-on rings of glass around the neck which were applied at first by hand and later made a part of the mold. We must remember that the molds used were unique in that they not only shaped the bottle, but patterned the surface as well. The fact that these decanters could be sold at a low price and made in quantity created important business for the glass houses producing them.

Many patterns were devised that were uniquely American. Flatter in design than cut glass, blown three-mold

decanters have an elegance in appearance that is unique. The patterns used range from simple ribbed design to the scroll motifs of the Baroque.

Attribution of blown three-mold glass is very difficult, as it is for much of the glass made up to 1850. There must have been many glass houses in the first half of the nineteenth century that continued to make only plain bottles and window glass and that stayed away from the risky business of manufacturing decorative glass, no matter how cheaply it could be made by this new method.

The Boston and Sandwich Glass Company, the Marlboro Street Factory at Keene, New Hampshire; the Mount Vernon Glass Company in New York, and the glass house at Coventry, Connecticut, are all known to have made blown three-mold glass. How many other firms made decanters and other glass articles in this unique manner might never be known. It is probable that some Ohio glass houses used three-part molds during this period.

Other sorts of bottles besides decanters were made in

LEFT: *Blown-three-mold decanter in pattern adapted from English cut glass. H. 8½ in.* Mattatuck

RIGHT: *Rare, square decanter in pint size made in two-part mold. Light aqua color. H. 7 in.* Mattatuck

FAR RIGHT: *Blown-three-mold decanter in sunburst, diamond, and rib pattern. Three double laid-on rings on neck. H. 7½ in.* Mattatuck

ABOVE: *Blown-three-mold decanter in "arch and fern" pattern. H. 8¼ in.* Mattatuck

RIGHT: *Ruby overlay on clear glass decanter. Triple-ringed neck. Possibly made at New England Glass Co. H. 9¼ in.* Mattatuck

blown three-mold patterns. Toilet bottles that were also used as camphor or vinegar containers were made in shades of blue, purple, green, and red as well as in milk glass. The most common color for these bottles, however, was clear.

Cruets and carafes were made as well as castor bottles, which were produced in matched sets of three, four or five pieces.

Many of the early decanters had no stoppers. The existing stoppers are sometimes interchangable, leading one to believe that a stopper was not made for each separate bottle pattern. Some of the stoppers were made of pressed glass, while others have blown-in-mold knobs.

The increasing use of pressed glass toward the middle of the nineteenth century led to the gradual abandonment of the blown three-mold process for decorative glass. Basically, the method for pressing glass by the use of a plunger into a mold was a process that did not require a glassblower's skill. Although this means of shaping glass objects had been used through the first half of

LEFT: *Blown-in-mold castor bottles. Pontil marks and flared lips. Clear glass. H. 4½ in. c. 1800.* Mattatuck

RIGHT: *"Bohemian" glass decanter. Clear glass with ruby overlay H. 9¼ in.* Mattatuck

Castor set with three-mold blown bottles and pressed glass stand. c. 1850. Author

the eighteenth century, it was not until 1830 that the Americans developed a more elaborate decoration by stippling the surface of the glass. Decanters could be made by this method that were more elaborate and brilliant and the style appealed to contemporary Victorian taste.

Chapter 12

BITTERS BOTTLES

WHILE a survey of the vast number of medicines and cures of the nineteenth century would lead the uninformed to believe that America was a nation of hypochondriacs, the truth is that a large proportion of the "medicine" taken by our Victorian forefathers was nothing more than flavored alcohol. There were few truly effective medications in those days, and the science of psychology was still in its infancy toward the end of the nineteenth century. America's panacea for pains and aches, both real and imagined, seems to have been a concoction called "bitters."

The practice of hiding one's alcoholic habit behind a façade of the medicine bottle was not an American phenomenon, however. Bitters had already been made in England, where George II's taxes on gin led enterprising pharmacists to make and bottle alcohol as medicine which could then be sold untaxed. In America, as the Victorian attitude toward alcohol grew and temperance became a cause, the guise of taking medicine which was supposedly

S.T.-1860-X.

DRAKE'S PLANTATION BITTERS

Invigorates, strengthens, and purifies the system; is a perfect appetizer, and Nature's great restorer. It is composed of pure St. Croix Rum, the celebrated Calisaya Bark, roots and herbs. Particularly adapted to weak and delicate persons, and can be relied upon for its purity. It cures Dyspepsia, is a gentle tonic, and is just the thing for changes of the seasons. Sold by all Grocers, Druggists, Hotels, and Saloons. P. H. Drake & Co. 202 Broadway, New York. s26 6ms

LEFT: *Dr. Pierce's Golden Medical Discovery. On back, "R. V. Pierce, M. D., Buffalo, N. Y." Aqua. H. 8¼ in.* Rebner

RIGHT: *Advertisement for popular bitters from New York Times, 1861.* Mattatuck

good for you protected many alcoholics from the wrath of their devoted spouses.

Since there were no laws against private enterprise in nineteenth-century America, wild claims could be made for the healthful qualities of bitters. There were also no laws that controlled the type or amount of ingredients that could be used. Bitters and other remedies could be mixed up and sold anywhere and anyone could call himself "Doctor."

The main ingredients in bitters were herbal extracts, used in small quantities for flavoring, and pure grain alcohol. Bitters created an alcoholic euphoria and while, obviously, they cured no one, particularly the alcoholic, they did make one indifferent to whatever had been ailing one . . . at least temporarily. For the most part, the curative powers of bitters were in the suggestive words of the pitchmen who touted them and in the persuasive advertisements that appeared with regularity in broadsides and newspapers.

Every ill that flesh is heir to had at least one concoction whose maker promised would cure it. Fictional "unsolicited testimonials" by the thousands promised miracle cures for everything from "bad blood" to jaundice. "Ben Hur Kidney and Liver Bitters," "Dr. Birmingham's Anti-Billious Blood Purifier Bitters," "Bismark Laxative Bitters," "Dandelion Blood Bitters," "E. Z. Laxative Bitters," "Dr. Manly Hardy's Genuine Jaundice Bitters," "Howe's Ague Cure and Tonic Bitters," "S. Kaufman's Celebrated Anti-Cholera Bitters," and "Poor Man's Bitters" are only a few of the names embossed on the early bottles or printed on the labels of these miraculous medications. There were thousands of different brands sold throughout the nation.

John Barleycorn came in the guise of cures of hundreds of self-styled "doctors," and many names of nineteenth-century bitters carried the onus of sobriety and medical righteousness. The miracle cures of "Dr. Hortenback," "Dr. Jacob," "Dr. Hoffman," "Dr. Hopkins," "Dr. Sweet," and many others give one an idea of what much of the "medical" profession was up to in the last

Three "story books" advertising bitters. Left: "My Lady's Mirror"—"Lady, be wise as you are fair/ Use Ayer's Vigor for the hair/ Fail not to heed this oracle/ Lest folly kill the follicle." Center: "The Witch Woman's Revenge" or "The Golden Secret of the Oswego." 1882, advertising Oswego Bitters at 25¢ a bottle. Right: "John, a Pastoral Poem" about a boy who after having been at death's door grew healthy and strong by taking Maltine with cod liver oil. Mattatuck

Full set of Handsome Lithographed Picture Cards free for 3 cents in Stamps
ADDRESS. FOSTER, MILBURN & CO. PROPRIETORS BUFFALO, N.Y.

THERE ARE AT LEAST FIVE THINGS THAT BURDOCK BLOOD BITTERS CAN DO AND WILL DO.

1. They will cure all weaknesses of the stomach, such as loss of appetite, indigestion and dyspepsia. If you want to eat a hearty meal, this is the medicine you need.

2. They will remove every vestige of disease from the blood, such as erysipelas, salt rheum, scrofula, chronic sores, pimples, blotches, etc., being an unexcelled purifying and strengthening medicine.

3. They will cure constipation, and sick headache in every instance of their use. Don't suffer from either of these troubles, when you have a perfect remedy in BURDOCK BLOOD BITTERS.

4. Thousands of people are steadily failing in health yet do not know what ails them. BURDOCK BLOOD BITTERS will cure this class of people. They will build up the wasted vital forces. Let no debilitated person fail to test them.

5. BURDOCK BLOOD BITTERS will convince the user of them that they stand in front and at the top of all proprietory and non-proprietory medicines. Try once.

For sale by every druggist.

FOSTER, MILBURN & CO., Mfrs. and Props.,

BUFFALO, N. Y.

Sold By H W Lake Druggist
Exchange Place.
Waterbury Conn.

Trade card for Burdock Blood Bitters. Mattatuck

LEFT: *Late bitters bottle made by Owen's machine. H. E. Buckley & Co., Chicago, Ill. Electric Brand Bitters. Dark amber. H. 8¾ in.* Rebner

RIGHT: *Dr. J. Hostetter's Stomach Bitters. Amber. H. 8¾ in.* Mattatuck

century. Before the invention of the real miracle drugs of this century there was little comfort to be given to a patient besides the relief that alcohol and narcotics brought. Genuine medical doctors were all too scarce in any case and alcoholic bitters all too available.

Bitters were made and sold in the late eighteenth century and throughout the nineteenth century, but the industry reached its zenith after 1862 when the Revenue Act caused liquor to be taxed. Bitters were also taxed, but less so than whiskey, and resentful citizens purchased more bitters than ever.

The Food and Drugs act restricted the sale of bitters as cures in 1906 and it became unlawful to ship or receive in interstate or foreign commerce any adulterated or misbranded food or drug. Once the amount of alcohol contained in a "medication" had to be printed on labels, the sale of bitters began to wane, but altered versions of the most popular brands continued to be manufactured and sold until around 1930.

Another factor that contributed to the control of the

ABOVE LEFT: *Dr. S. O. Richardson's Bitters, South Reading, Massachusetts. Blown-in-mold aqua bottle. H. 5 in.* Rebner

ABOVE RIGHT: *Embossed "Cocamoke Bitter Co./Hartford/ Conn." Dark amber. H 9½ in.* Rebner

RIGHT: *"Atwood's Jaundice bitters/formerly made by/ Moses Atwood/ Georgetown, Mass," Paneled pale aqua bottle. H. 6 in.* Rebner

amount of alcohol in beverages of medical quacks was the effort of the Woman's Temperance Crusade of 1873-74. The W. C. T. U. carried on a long and arduous campaign to abolish the sale of liquor in any form in the United States. There is little doubt, however, that many of these same virtuous and well-meaning women swore by a variety of cures for female ills that were bottled and advertised just for them. The ladies knew what was good for them, and a good part of it was pure grain alcohol!

Bitters bottles as collectible relics of the past are important in the history of two major American industries, the bottle industry and the patent medicine business. The development of special kinds of glass bottles and the enormous popularity of bitters led to a burgeoning of the glass bottle industry in America. Whereas in the early part of the nineteenth century whiskey had been bottled and sold in flasks that did not vary too much in their basic shape, bitters bottles were designed with more practical needs in mind. Bitters was sold as medicine, so the

Paper wrapper on this aqua bottle advertises Vinegar Bitters made in San Francisco. Clear. H. 8½ in. Mattatuck

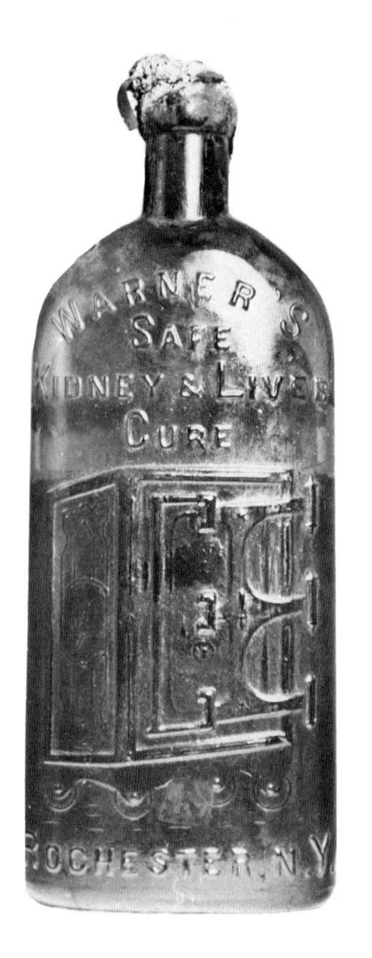

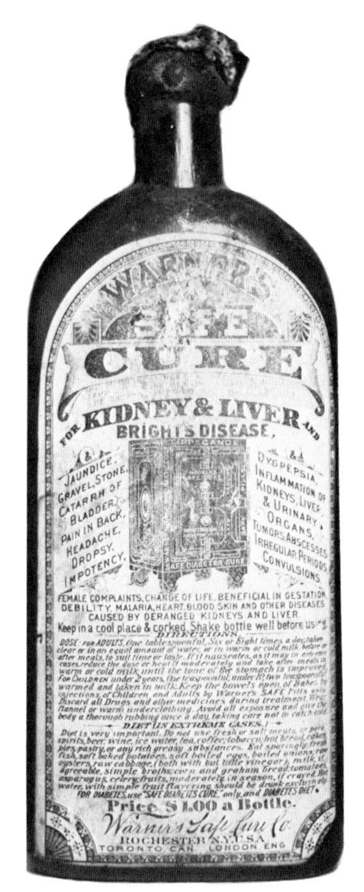

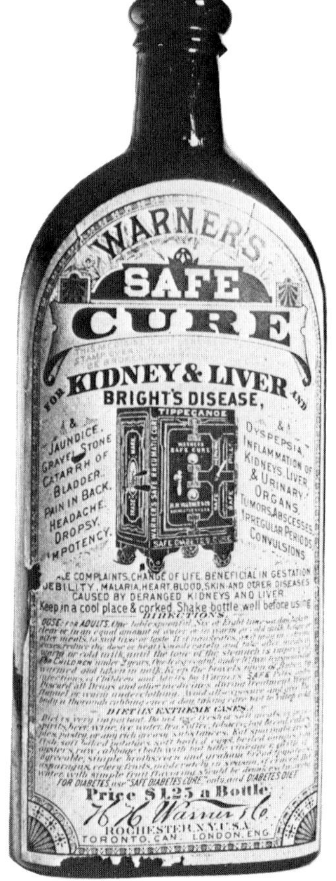

Three versions of "Warner's Safe Cure Bitters." LEFT: *Embossed bottle showing safe.* CENTER: *Later bottle showing no embossment and label. Note price at $1.00.* RIGHT: *On still later bottle, price has increased by 25%. All bottles h. 10 in.* Mattatuck bottles were usually smaller and made in a shape that would pack easily for transportation. They were usually rectangular or square, and packed in boxes of a dozen; round bottles were also made. It was natural that as the bitters industry became more competitive, bottles that would have distinctive shapes were designed. Flask shapes were rarely used since the connection in the public's eye with whiskey would have been all too revealing. There were only two flask shapes made.

Most bitters bottles are easily identified since the names of the remedies are embossed on the glass. Later, labels were a means of identification and because more printed information could be put on labels longer lists of illnesses that the maker claimed his brand would cure were found on them.

Bitters bottle collectors search for labeled as well as embossed bottles. The wildest claims for the powers of bitters were made in every medium available at the time. Outdoor signs, trade cards, catalogs, and almanacs were all used to promote the many brands of bitters available.

Old malt bitters bottle showing original label and seal. Green. H. 9 in. Mattatuck

Since bitters was a product with which many of the European groups settling in America had not been unfamiliar in their own countries, efforts were made to label bitters in their native languages or to give many brands fake ethnic names that would appeal to the immigrant groups.

The Shaker communities were not above bottling their own brands of bitters which were advertised for sale to the outside world. These were advertised in Shaker printed almanacs and catalogs that included a few recipes and advertisements for other Shaker products as well.

As the bitters industry grew toward the middle of the nineteenth century, bottle manufacturers began to design bottles in shapes that would be easily identified with one brand of bitters. It is this variety of shapes as well as colors that make bitters bottles one of the most interesting to the collector. Bottles with geometric designs, roped embellishments, decorative panels, diaper patterns, ribbing, fluting, and embossed pictures and patterns soon gave way to figural bottles of many types. Barrels, drums,

fish, and log-cabins are only a few of the shapes of the bitters bottles that were made.

Blown-in-mold bitters bottles, made in glass of aquamarine, green, clear, blue, and puce are among the most collectible of old American bottles. However, all bitters bottles of the nineteenth century are interesting to history buffs and bottle collectors. The early advertisements and wild claims printed on trade cards and almanacs are collateral material.

A popular bitters, Dr. Harter's, complied with Pure Food and Drug Laws in 1906. Note revised formula still has 24% alcohol. Bottle dark amber. H. 7½ in. Mattatuck

TOP: *Buchan's Hungarian "Balsam of Life." Dark amber. H. 6 in.* Mattatuck

BELOW LEFT: *Embossed on side panels: "Rev. N. A. Downs' Vegetable Balsamic Elixir." Light aqua. Twelve-paneled bottle. H. 4½ in.* Mattatuck

RIGHT: *Halls Balsam for the lungs. Pale blue. H. 8 in.* Mattatuck

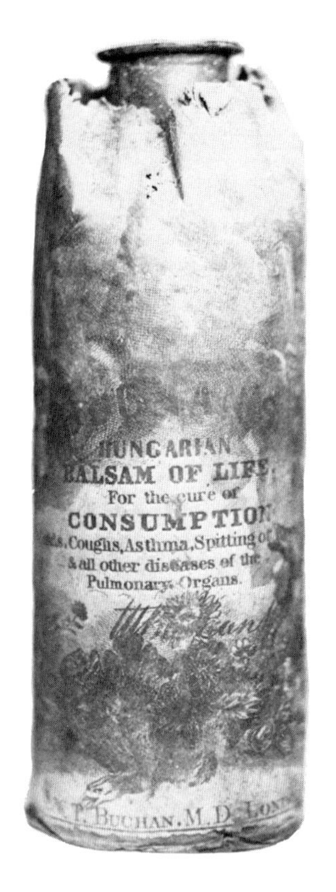

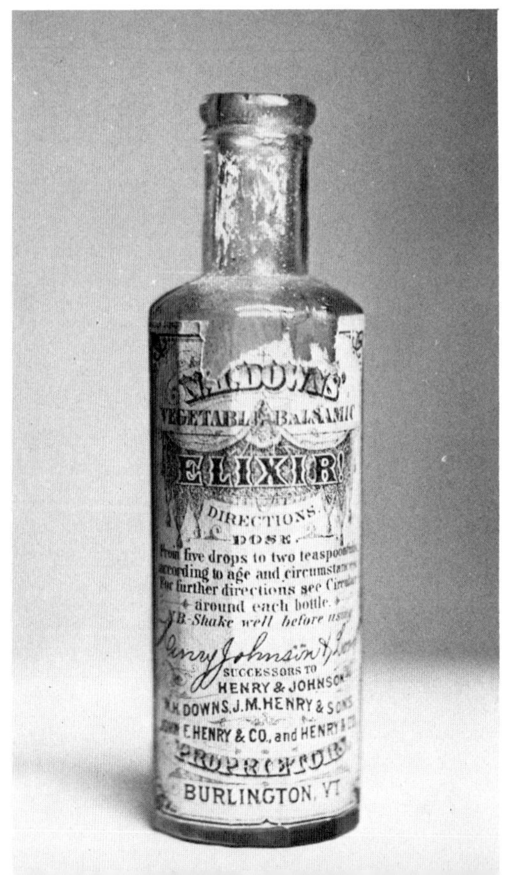

Chapter 13

PATENT MEDICINE BOTTLES

WHILE bitters was an alcoholic drink sold as a medicine, there were hundreds of other medicines that were not called "bitters" that were sold during the nineteenth century and advertised as curing every disease known to man and animal. Many of these medicines contained alcohol, opium, morphine, and other harmful ingredients. There was often no way to know what was put in these concoctions and no law to control what went into them. Furthermore, they were often mixed in dirty pots in any backyard or barn under conditions that were far from sanitary.

Mothers were induced to lull their restless children to sleep with soothing syrups containing opium or other harmful drugs. Comforting names such as "Mrs. Winslow's Soothing Syrup" or "Infant's Friend" contributed to the high mortality rate of children and probably crippled and addicted many more.

There was no adult sickness, either, for which there was no cure. Sarsaparilla syrups with alcohol were generally touted as curing syphilis, a disease that must have

Dr. Haynes' Arabian Balsam. Light aqua. twelve-paneled. Front and rear view. H. 4 in.
Hardy

been rampant, judging from the many brands of sarsaparilla that were made.

Druggists and charlatans who called themselves "doctor" bottled their remedies, many of which became popular enough to be sold throughout the country in enormous amounts. Other remedies were purely local and were often made and sold by the town druggist. Often the same people who produced and bottled bitters made a brand of sarsaparilla as well as other medicines.

In the nineteenth century there were hundreds of products that restored hair to gleaming pates (or claimed to); consumption could be cured by drinking any one of thousands of syrups; blood could be purified as quickly as one could say "Marshall's Concentrated Compound Syrup of Sarsaparilla." Smaller dosages for children were sometimes, although not always, recommended. Special elixirs for females and "pain extractors" were advertised and sold; and asthma, kidney and liver troubles, rheumatism, diabetes, fever, and ague could all be abolished by many different remedies.

ABOVE: *Dr. Wistar's Balsam of Wild Cherry, Phila. Eight panels. Aqua. H. 6¼ in.* Rebner

ABOVE LEFT: *Trade card for Dr. Wistar's Balsam of Wild Cherry.* Mattatuck

LEFT: *Dr. Browder's Compound Syrup of Indian Turnip.* Mattatuck

FAR LEFT: *Dr. Blanchard Concentrated Blood and Nerve Food. Embossed on shoulders of bottle. "Food" and "Cure." Amber. H. 6½ in.* Mattatuck Rebner

DR A. BOSCHEE'S
GERMAN SYRUP

PULMONIC

MRS E. KIDDER
DYSENTERY
CORDIAL
BOSTON

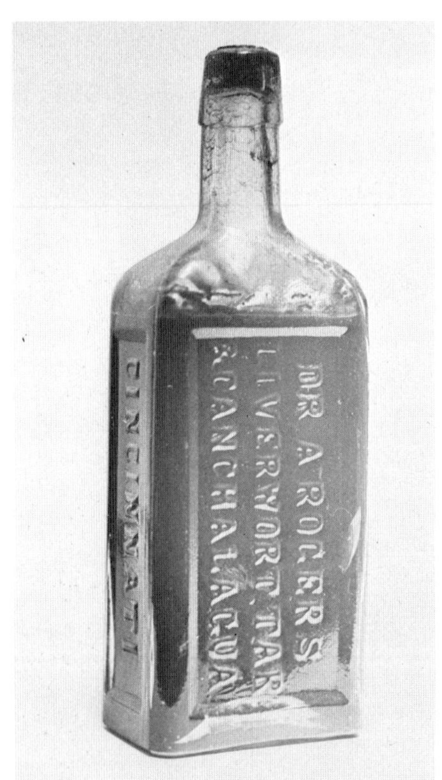
CINCINNATI
DR A. ROGERS
LIVERWORT, TAR
& CANCHALAGUA

COMPOUND SYRUP OF
LIVERWORT, TAR
AND
CANCHALAGUA
GENUINE ALWAYS SIGNED
NEW-YORK

OPPOSITE PAGE

TOP LEFT: *Dr. Boschee's German Syrup. Light medium green. H. 6¾ in.* Rebner

CENTER: *Schenk's Pulmonic Syrup. Philadelphia. Aqua. H. 6½ in.* Rebner

RIGHT: *Mrs. E. Kidder's Dysentery Cordial, Boston. Pale aqua. H. 8 in.* Mattatuck

BOTTOM PAIR: *Dr. A. Rogers/ Liverwort tar/ & Canchalagua/ Cincinnati. View with label. Dark aqua. H. 7¾ in.* Mattatuck

THIS PAGE

TOP LEFT: *Double collared medicine bottle in amber, embossed "celery compound."* Mattatuck

RIGHT: *Davis Cholera Remedy. Clear glass. H. 5 in.* Mattatuck

BOTTOM LEFT: *After Food and Drugs Act all alcoholic medications had to state percentage of alcohol on label. Clear glass. H. 5½ in.* Mattatuck

RIGHT: *Upham's Fresh Meat Cure. Clear glass. H. 7 in.* Mattatuck

ABOVE LEFT: *Dr. D. Kennedy's Favorite Remedy. Kingston, N. Y. Aqua. H. 8¼ in.*

ABOVE RIGHT: *Dr. J. W. Bull's Vegetable Baby Syrup. Unusual round bottle. Clear glass. H. 5 in.* Mattatuck

RIGHT: *Three light aqua sarsaparilla bottles. This root flavor was used as base syrup for many medicines. Eventually it became a soft drink. Center bottle. H. 9⅛ in.* Rebner

The great patent medicine era was far from great for the truly sick or those who proved to be easily addicted to alcohol or narcotics. The popular panaceas made many fake doctors extremely rich. The medicine man who followed the frontier touting his brands of cures and entertaining the crowds raked in a lot of money on false promises. Even the great catalog stores of the late nineteenth century had their own brands of cures and tonics that were sent through the mail. In an era not far removed from the belief that blood-letting would lead to recovery from most illnesses, the hope of getting well by drinking any of the thousands of patent medicines offered was, perhaps, a step forward in medical annals.

The use of home-made medicine goes far back in medical history. However, the general sale of patent remedies began in England in the eighteenth century. British remedies were sold in the colonies before the Revolutionary War and it was during the war that American know-how took over in the field of commercially made remedies. Closely allied to the medi-

LEFT: *Trade card for Hood's Sarsaparilla.* Mattatuck

RIGHT: *"Genuine Sands' Sarsaparilla" Made in New York. Aqua bottle. H 9¾ in.* Rebner

RIGHT: *Sarsaparilla bottle in original paper wrapper.*
Mattatuck

BELOW: *Scott's Emulsion with lime and soda and cod liver oil. Light green. H. 9 in.*
Rebner

cine business was the growth of advertising in America. Medicine was among the first American products widely advertised in newspapers, Affidavits and testimonials in the early advertisements attest to the high quality of the medicines and many fictional satisfied customers claimed that a tonic or elixir saved their lives.

Small books that were either given away or sold for a penny or two were issued extolling a particular brand of medicine. One tells of how a secret formula for a remedy was given to the manufacturer by an Indian known for his strength and vitality. A common story would be how the narrator was at death's door until he discovered Dr. So-and-so's miraculous remedy which not only restored him to health, but gave him an appetite he had never previously had and made his hair grow in thick and lustrous.

Wild and false claims were made over and over and they gave the terminally ill new hope. If one remedy did not work, one could always try another. There was a seemingly endless source of supply.

ABOVE: *Embossed on other side of this bottle in ribbon is "Citrate of Magnesia" Porcelain stopper. Light aqua. H. 8 in.* Mattatuck

BELOW: *Advertisements for medicines made wild claims and helped sell a lot of medicine.* Mattatuck

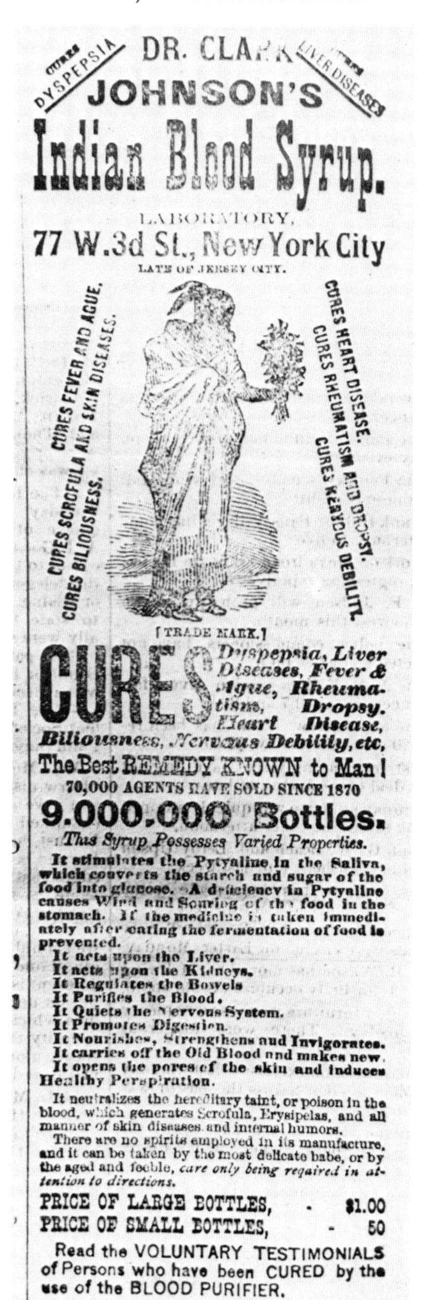

CURES DYSPEPSIA
DR. CLARK
CURES LIVER DISEASES
JOHNSON'S
Indian Blood Syrup.
LABORATORY,
77 W. 3d St., New York City
LATE OF JERSEY CITY.
CURES FEVER AND AGUE.
CURES SCROFULA AND SKIN DISEASES.
CURES BILIOUSNESS.
CURES HEART DISEASE.
CURES RHEUMATISM AND DROPSY.
CURES NERVOUS DEBILITY.
[TRADE MARK.]
CURES Dyspepsia, Liver Diseases, Fever & Ague, Rheumatism, Dropsy. Heart Disease, Biliousness, Nervous Debility, etc,
The Best REMEDY KNOWN to Man!
70,000 AGENTS HAVE SOLD SINCE 1870
9.000.000 Bottles.
This Syrup Possesses Varied Properties.
It stimulates the Pytyaline in the Saliva, which converts the starch and sugar of the food into glucose. A deficiency in Pytyaline causes Wind and Souring of the food in the stomach. If the medicine is taken immediately after eating the fermentation of food is prevented.
It acts upon the Liver.
It acts upon the Kidneys.
It Regulates the Bowels
It Purifies the Blood.
It Quiets the Nervous System.
It Promotes Digestion.
It Nourishes, Strengthens and Invigorates.
It carries off the Old Blood and makes new.
It opens the pores of the skin and induces Healthy Perspiration.
It neutralizes the hereditary taint, or poison in the blood, which generates Scrofula, Erysipelas, and all manner of skin diseases and internal humors.
There are no spirits employed in its manufacture, and it can be taken by the most delicate babe, or by the aged and feeble, care only being required in attention to directions.
PRICE OF LARGE BOTTLES, - $1.00
PRICE OF SMALL BOTTLES, - 50
Read the VOLUNTARY TESTIMONIALS of Persons who have been CURED by the use of the BLOOD PURIFIER.

RIGHT: *Snuff was sold as a medication as well as for the nicotine "high." Bottle is aqua. H. 4½ in.* Rebner

RIGHT: *Trade card for St. Jacob's Oil.* Mattatuck

BELOW: *Trade card for Allan's Beef, Wine and Iron Tonic. A view of Narragansett Bay in Rhode Island.* Mattatuck

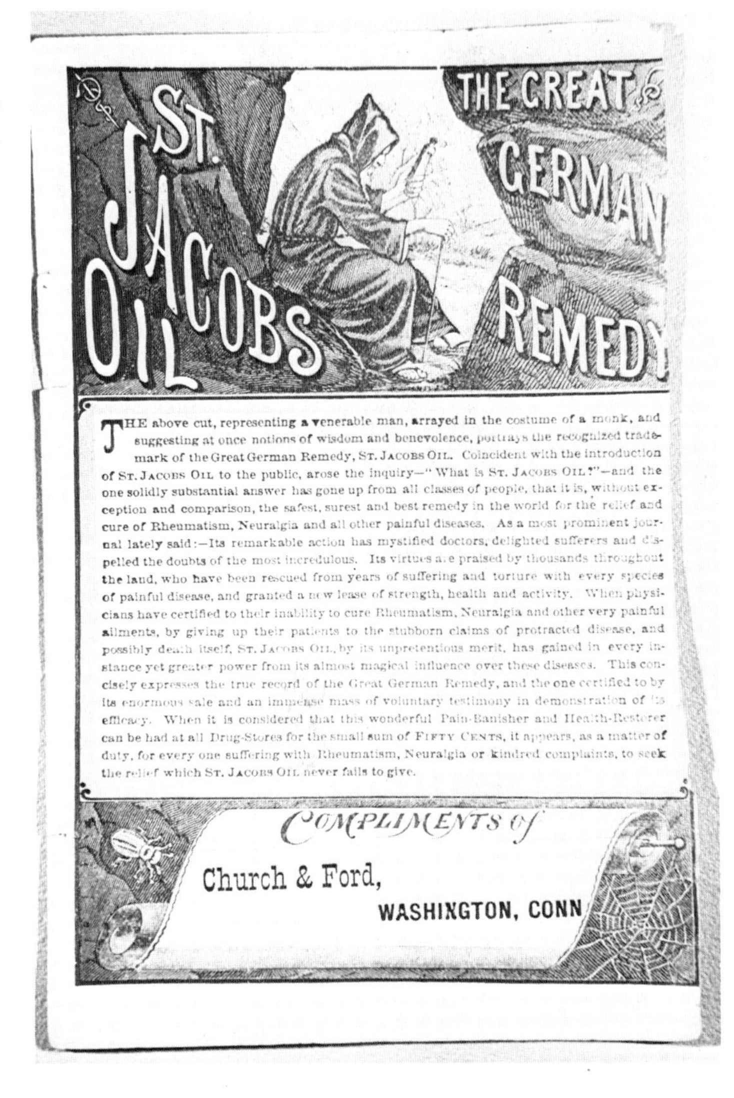

OUR 60-CENT PRINCESS HAIR RESTORER.

No. 8R1101

Per Bottle, 60c.

THE PRINCESS WORLD FAMED HAIR TONIC RESTORER

SEARS, ROEBUCK & CO. Cheapest Supply House on Earth WE SELL EVERYTHING

CHICAGO ILL.

PRINCESS HAIR RESTORER IS GOOD FOR BOTH

A WONDERFUL NEW HAIR TONIC AND PRODUCER.

Restores the Natural Color, Preserves and Strengthens the Hair for Years, Promotes the Growth, Arrests Falling Hair, Feeds an Nourishes the Roots, Cures Dandruff and Scurf, and Allays all Scalp Irritations.

Regular Retail Price, per bottle, $1.0
Our Price, per bottle, ...6
Our Price, per dozen 6.0

Unmailable on account of weight.

The only absolutely effective, unfailingly successful, perfectly harmless, positively no-dye preparation on the market that restores gray hair to its natural and youthful color, removes crusts, scales and dandruff, soothes irritating, itching surfaces, stimulates the hair follicles, supplies the roots with energy and nourishment, renders the hair beautifully soft, and makes the hair grow WHEN ALL ELSE FAILS.

EVERY SINGLE BOTTLE OF PRINCESS HAIR RESTORER is compounded especially in our own laboratory by our own skilled chemists, and according to the prescription of one who has made the hair and scalp, its diseases and cure, a life study.

PRINCESS HAIR RESTORER IS NOT AN EXPERIMENT, not an untried unknown, quack remedy, depending on enormous, glittering advertisements for sales, but it is a preparation of the very finest and most expensive ingredients that will positively cure any case of falling hair, stimulate the growth of new hair on bald heads, cure dandruff and other diseases of the scalp.

ARE YOU BALD?

IS YOUR HAIR THIN OR FALLING OUT?

DOES YOUR HAIR COME OUT EASILY AND GATHER ON THE COMB AND BRUSH WHEN YOU BRUSH IT?

DOES YOUR HEAD ITCH?

DO YOU HAVE DANDRUFF OR SCURF AND DO WHITE, DUST-LIKE PARTICLES SETTLE ON YOUR COAT COLLAR?

IS YOUR HAIR STIFF AND COARSE AND HARD TO BRUSH?

IS YOUR HAIR FADING OR HAS IT TURNED PREMATURELY GRAY?

IF YOUR HAIR SUFFERS in any one or more of these particulars, we would urge you by all means to order a bottle of **Princess Hair Restorer** as a trial, for speedy relief. Use it according to directions and you will be surprised and delighted at the wonderful results. **PRINCESS HAIR RESTORER NEVER FAILS.** It acts direct on the tiny roots of the hair, giving them required fresh nourishment, starts quick and energetic circulation in every hair cell, tones up the scalp, freshens the pores, stops falling and sickly hair, changes thin hair to a fine heavy growth, puts new life in dormant, sluggish hair cells on bald heads, producing in a short time an **absolutely new growth of hair. If your hair is fading or turning gray,** one bottle of Princess Hair Restorer will give it healthy life, renew its original color and restore it to youthful profusion and beauty.

USE IT ALWAYS IF YOU WANT A HEAD OF FINE, SILKY, GLOSSY HAIR, THE PRIDE OF EVERY WOMAM.

Princess Hair Restorer Grows Hair Like This.

AS A CURE FOR DANDRUFF, **as a tonic for thin and scanty hair, Princess Hair Restorer acts with quick and wonderfu success.** It removes crusts and scales, keeps the scalp clean and healthy, the roots at once respond to its vigorous action, dandruff is banished and a thick and healthy growth of hair is assured.

FOR A TOILET ARTICLE, **as a fine hair dressing,** no one who takes any pride in a nice head of hair can afford to be without a bottle always on the dresser. **Princess Hair Restorer** is delicately perfumed, and one light application imparts a delightful, refined fragrance. Neither oils, pomades, vaseline or other greases are require with our preparation.

TOP: *Sears Roebuck advertisement for hair restorer from 1902 Catalogue.*

BOTTOM LEFT: *Bottle for hair restorer which was also good for the skin.* Rebner

RIGHT: *J. R. Birdsall's Arnica Liniment. Light aqua bottle.* Rebner

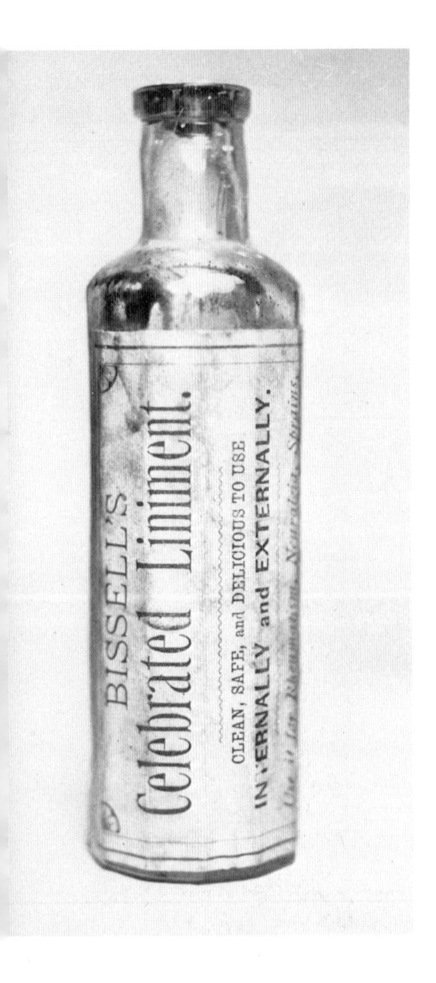

LEFT: *Bissell's Celebrated Liniment for Horses and Cattle. Light aqua. H. 3½ in.*
Mattatuck

RIGHT: *Merchant's Celebrated Gargling Oil for Horses and Cattle. Green. H. 7½ in.*
Mattatuck

The American Indian was not the only ethnic group credited with the secret of the restoration of health through the release of "secret formulae." The Chinese, Germans, and various South American peoples gave an aura of authenticity to some of the medications, for example "Dr. Lin's Celestial Balm of China." Many other exotic names were used to convince the buyer that he was in good medical hands. Every symbol that bespoke strength and well-being was used to sell patent medicine. Methods of advertising and promotion were almost as numerous as the brands of medicines that were sold—or the illnesses that they were supposed to cure. The pitchman came on the scene with stories of miraculous cures, and many had testimonials from members of their audience who swore that what he said was the truth.

Charlatans were the rule rather than the exception in the manufacture of patent medicine. The lack of legal control over harmful ingredients made it easy to go into a business that was lucrative and required very little investment. There were thousands of patent medicines being made by 1900, a great proportion of them containing alcohol and harmful drugs. The Pure Food and Drug Act of 1906 put an end to the masses of medicines that had been sold and the more harmful ones were taken off the market. Some of the more popular medicines were altered to comply with the law and these were sold after 1906. However, many of these did not sell well once the harmful ingredients, alcohol or narcotics, were removed. They had lost their potency.

Collectors of patent and proprietary medicine bottles are especially interested in those with embossments such as the amusing names of the medicine or the maker and his address. Early patent medicine bottles with labels intact are finds for the collector. In many cases paper wrappers were used rather than labels or boxes. Age and the evidence of pontil marks and sheared lips are particularly desirable in medicine bottles, but unusual shapes and colors are less important than the embossing.

The patent medicine era is well documented in early newspaper advertisements, almanacs, small story books,

LEFT: *Humphreys' Homeopathic Veterinary Specifics. Horse Liniment. Clear glass. Embossment of laughing horse. H. 3½. 1868.* Mattatuck

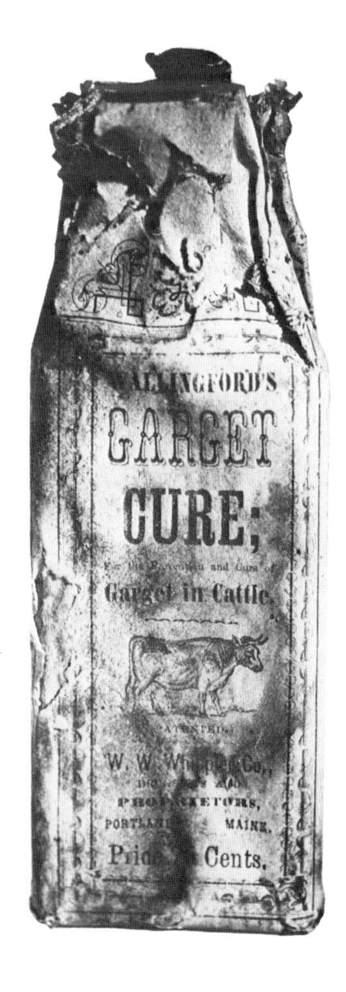

RIGHT: *Another medication for ailing cattle. At least these patients could not complain. Clear. H. 6 in.* Mattatuck

Advertisement from 1902 Sears catalogue. "Somone" undoubtedly contained narcotics and worked very well.

If by mail, postage extra, per box, small, 2 cents; large, 4 cents.

Somone, for Sweet, Refreshing Sleep.

Retail price.......................................$1.50
Our price, each..................................$0.67
Our price, per dozen..............................6.00

A RELIABLE REMEDY FOR SLEEPLESSNESS. We ask any of our customers **who may be troubled with insomnia, who cannot sleep at night, to give this valuable remedy a trial.** No matter from what cause the sleeplessness arises, a sound sleep will be procured by its use, and you will awake in the morning refreshed, strengthened and cheerful; no bad effects from its use. We guarantee it to contain no opium, morphine or poisonous narcotics of any kind whatever. It is a vegetable preparation composed of herbs soothing and healing to the entire system. It can be used in safety by the weakest and most delicate and is a boon to those of nervous dispositions. A single dose will strengthen and invigorate them and cause them to forget their troubles. Ladies troubled with nervous spells should always have a bottle at hand. A dose or two in time will save them many hours of agony and serious discomfort and often prevent total collapse of the nervous system. It has a marvelous effect on those afflicted with nervous prostration, acting like magic in restoring the nerves to their normal condition and causing a strong healthy feeling to prevail throughout the whole body. It quiets the nervous excitement and muscular trembling caused by the excessive use of liquor, and acts as an antidote to the liquor habit. Full directions accompany each bottle how to use it both for sleeplessness and nervous troubles.

DO NOT FAIL TO INCLUDE THIS REMEDY IN YOUR QUANTITY ORDER. THOUSANDS OF PATIENTS NEED IT AND BUY IT.

SOMONE

and trade cards. The colorful posters used by the pitchmen are more difficult to find. Nineteenth-century relics of the patent medicine days have long been of interest to bottle collectors, to whom the story of the great American medical hoax is a fascinating part of our history.

Chapter 14

DRUGSTORE BOTTLES

THE early drugstore of America holds a great deal of nostalgia for the historian as well as the collector. The local pharmacist often had as much or more training in medicine than the town doctor—when there was one. It was not unusual for the pharmacist to prescribe and advise, and most proprietors of drugstores in eighteenth- and nineteenth-century America were given the honorary and affectionate title of "Doc." Few, if any, pharmacists ever refuted this title and many of them used it professionally when they made and bottled their own medicines. In an era when the medical profession was struggling to set up standards by which to judge itself, there was no one to prevent the unethical use of the title. In many cases, physicians made their own medications and pharmacists treated the sick.

Bottles made for use by apothecaries of the eighteenth and nineteenth centuries have been desirable to collectors for many years. The earliest American glass houses made phials and jars for the storage of chemicals, herbs, and other ingredients that were mixed together by the local

View of apothecary shop of nineteenth century.
Mattatuck

physician or apothecary. Before the Revolutionary War many of these glass drug bottles were made in England, but the interruption of the War caused American glass houses to provide supplies in this country. Dr. Dyott lists for sale "Vials, ½ to 8 oz." and many other kinds of druggist wares as early as 1818. Many types of patent medicine bottles were also made at Kensington at that time.

There are many different types of collectible drugstore bottles from which to choose. The most desirable of these are the apothecary jars and bottles made for permanent storage of the hundreds of powders, chemicals and herbs that were necessary for the prescription medicines. Although the use of apothecary jars goes back many centuries in Europe, those that can be found today in this country are nineteenth-century bottles, and many have enameled, printed or painted labels. Some have recessed panels on which a printed label was affixed and covered with glass. Bottles of the latter type were made after 1862.

Apothecary jars have long been considered attractive enough to use decoratively. Many have ground-glass stoppers that fit the bottles perfectly to prevent evaporation of the contents. Some of these reusable bottles have embossed labels rather than the attractive printed or painted labels while others are unlabeled.

Other drugstore bottles that may be collected are the phials made by the old glass houses and the bottles and

LEFT: *Group of early blown-glass drug bottles.* Mattatuck

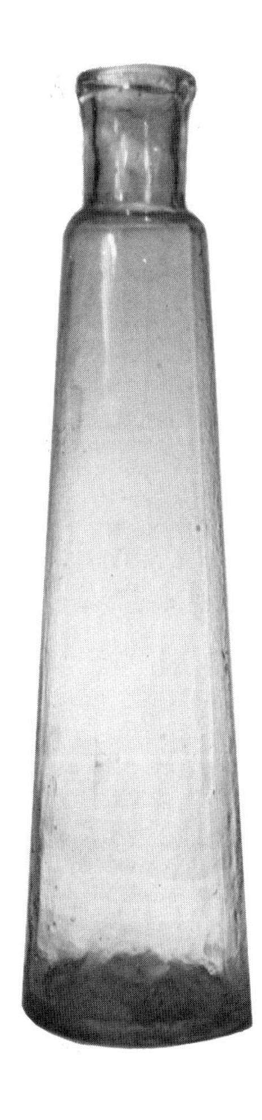

RIGHT: *Drug bottle from First's Drug Store, Middlebury, Vermont. Made by Old Dunsmore Glass Works of Vermont. Light aqua. Pontil scar. H. 5½ in.* Mattatuck

ABOVE LEFT: *Embossed apothecary bottle with monogram. Aqua. H. 7 in.* Mattatuck

ABOVE RIGHT: *Apothecary bottle in cobalt blue glass. Ground stopper and ground pontil. H. 9 in.* Hardy

RIGHT: *Group of apothecary bottles with paper labels.*

TOP: *Clear glass apothecary jar with recessed label covered with glass panel. Embossed on bottom: Warren Glass Works, New York and Cumberland, Md. H. 9 in.* Hardy

BOTTOM PAIR: *Two chemist's bottles, "Wyeth & Bro., Phila.": one is clear glass, the other cobalt blue.* Mattatuck

Hazard & Caswell, Newport, Chemists. Aqua. Three bottles show succession of partners and locations of firm. H. 10 in. Rebner

jars used to store or mix drugs. Many of these pieces of early glass have pontil marks and most are in the pale aqua color. Bottles from the nineteenth-century drug supply houses are also collected. These often have embossments of the name of the firm and its location as well as an accompanying monogram.

Tablet jars, tooth powder jars, and prescription bottles are highly collectible. Medicine bottles made in plate molds with the name of the druggist and other embossments are especially favored by collectors. The invention of the plate mold in the 1880s made it possible for standard sized medicine bottles to be made with names embossed at very little expense. Most of the smaller drugstores ordered plate-mold bottles, while the larger stores had bottle molds made especially for them with embossing and shapes that were more individualized. Some of these embossments feature symbols of the apothecary such as mortars and pestles or store monograms.

The apothecary's symbol during the nineteenth century was the large fancy apothecary jar filled with col-

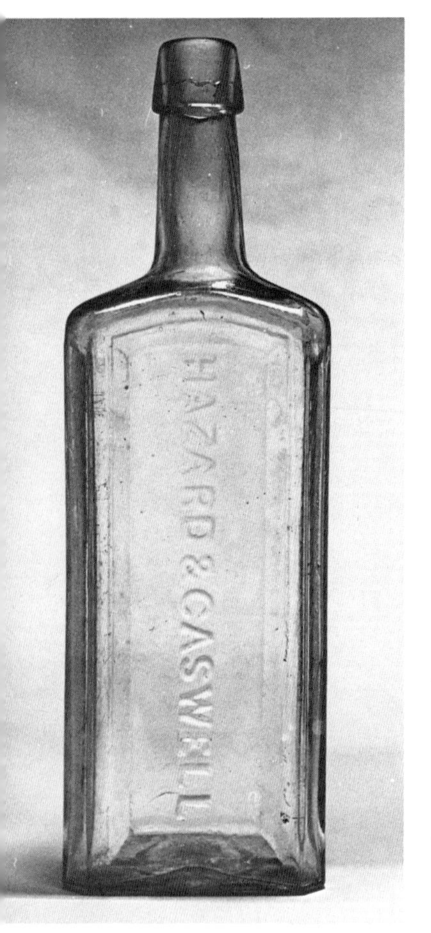

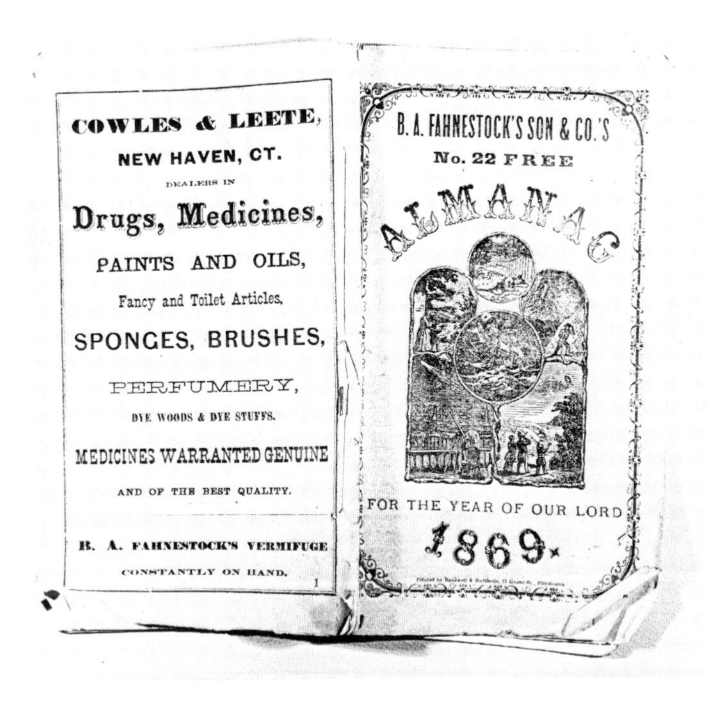

COWLES & LEETE,
NEW HAVEN, CT.
DEALERS IN
Drugs, Medicines,
PAINTS AND OILS,
Fancy and Toilet Articles,
SPONGES, BRUSHES,
PERFUMERY,
DYE WOODS & DYE STUFFS.
MEDICINES WARRANTED GENUINE
AND OF THE BEST QUALITY.
B. A. FAHNESTOCK'S VERMIFUGE
CONSTANTLY ON HAND.
1
B. A. FAHNESTOCK'S SON & CO.'S
No. 22 FREE
ALMANAC
FOR THE YEAR OF OUR LORD
1869.

TOP: *Druggists issued almanacs every year which contained advertisements for their medicines.* Mattatuck

BELOW LEFT: *Embossed apothecary bottle with monogram.* Rebner

RIGHT: *Two drug bottles. Bottle on left is embossed with dots so that it can be distinguished in the dark. It is probably a poison bottle. H. 5⅛ in. Bottle on right is light aqua. H. 4½ in.* Mattatuck

TOP: *Advertisement from nineteenth-century newspaper for apothecary's own brand of medicine.* Mattatuck

BOTTOM: *Apothecary's trade card.* Mattatuck

au19dawtf

Apothecaries.

WORM KILLER.

FOR the destruction of all the **various forms** of worms that infest the stomach and bowels, except tape worms.

It is purely vegetable and pleasant to take and will not injure the youngest child.

☞ 25c a bottle, sold by sole agent,

J. O. Wild, Apothecary

Abbott's Building.

EUREKA PRINT, NEW HAVEN
BRIGGS & HIGBY,
APOTHECARIES,
Cor. North and East Main Streets,
Waterbury, Conn.

Doctor's box with bottles of powders for mixing medicines in the patients' homes. c. 1850.
Marie Whitney Antiques

ored water. Just as the tobacconist used the cigar store Indian and the barber the striped pole, the apothecary placed a tall jar filled with colored water in his shop window. These window jars came in a variety of shapes and were always very elaborate and decorative. Since there were not as many of these made as there were apothecary jars, they are scarce today.

Among the most desirable of all drugstore bottles are those that contained poison. These special bottles were made in an attempt to avoid tragic accidents by putting all poisonous liquids into easily identifiable bottles. Embossments making the bottle rough to the touch and often with the word "poison" were two methods of identification. Quite often, also, the bottle was made in cobalt blue glass. Skull and crossbones were used as symbols and a few bottles were made in the shape of a coffin. Various types of safety closures were invented for these bottles also. The majority of poison bottles that can be found today date between 1870 and 1930. Shape, embossments,

Cobalt blue Bromo Seltzer bottle. Emerson Drug Co. Baltimore, Md. H. 4 in.
Rebner

and unusual colors are all features that make these bottles desirable for collectors.

There is a great deal of collateral material for the collector of drugstore bottles. Advertisements and the many drugstore items such as mortars and pestles, scales, drug records, and prescription pads are all collected. Doctor's boxes fitted with old bottles for mixing medicines at the patient's house are also interesting and decorative. The nostalgia for the old corner drugstore has made many people collect items that were once a part of the American scene, and drug bottles are among the memorabilia highly prized.

Chapter 15

BEER BOTTLES

THERE was no shortage of beer in the early days of America. Everyone was his own brewer. Directions for "fitting up a small brewhouse" to make beer for home consumption were given in an early nineteenth-century "receipt" book. Thirty-five recipes for beer and ale are given, including one for making beer from pea shells.

Local commercial breweries began to sprout up at the beginning of the nineteenth century wherever an area was populated enough to support them. By mid-century there were over 400 breweries in the United States. Beer was put up in barrels for local distribution. When it was packaged in bottles it would spoil within a matter of days before the development of effective closures. The lack of easy transportation contributed to the growth of so many regional breweries. When the railroads were built toward the end of the nineteenth century, this problem was solved for the brewers. In 1850 there were only 9,000 miles of railroads in operation, all of them in the

Aachener Kaiser Brunnen. Inside screw-thread stopper. Green glass. H. 10¾ in.
Rebner

East. By 1890 the vast network of railroads had been completed across the nation.

There were two problems that stood in the way of packaging beer in bottles in the latter half of the nineteenth century. The first had to do with spoilage. Louis Pasteur's studies of fermentation in wine and beer and his subsequent discovery of a process to prevent spoilage by the use of heat solved this first problem for the brewers. The research that was started to save the French wine industry proved to be a boon to the brewers as well.

The other problem was the lack of a suitable and functional bottle closure. Many different methods were tried. The "Lightning" stopper became the most widely used method of closing beer bottles throughout the nineteenth century. In 1892, William Painter revolutionized the bottle industry by inventing the cork-lined crown cap.

The bottled beer industry did not really grow to the proportions that we now know until the invention of Owen's bottle machine, when uniform bottles could be

YOU'LL NEVER MISS THE LAGER TIL THE KEG RUNS DRY.
COPYRIGHTED, BUFFORD, BOSTON

C. CORRIGAN,

DEALER IN

Ales, Wines, Liquors,

and Lager Beer,

Cigars, Tobacco, &c.

Rob't Smith's Philadelphia Stock Ales and Porter.

LEFT: *Trade card for liquor dealer. Late nineteenth century.* Mattatuck

ABOVE: *Beadleston & Woerz, Empire Brewery, N. Y. Around base of bottle. "This bottle not to be sold." Aqua. H. 9 in.* Rebner

Beer bottle, amber, applied crown cap neck. Etched wreath of leaves halfway up bottle. H. 9¼ in. Rebner

used with Painter's crown cap. But another curtailment on the industry was that Federal law had provision for taxing kegged beer only and, therefore, the internal revenue stamp could only be placed on kegs. This meant that the brewers had to own or contract for separate bottling plants where they had to send the kegs to be opened after they had been taxed. This law was not changed until 1890 when the financial burden of packaging beer twice was lifted from the brewers.

Until 1840 ale, porter, and stout, made in the British tradition, were the types of beer consumed in America. With the influx of German immigrants to this country in the mid-nineteenth century, lager beer, which is fermented differently from British beers, was introduced and gained in popularity. Since all breweries at the time were local, regional beer types reflected the type of community they served.

Collectors of early beer bottles tend to become involved with American history and geography. Many of the embossed bottles that are marked with the brewer's

Ironstone brewery mug with printed monogram of company under glaze. Author

name have the address as well. Since local brewers sprang up shortly after towns became established and many went out of business rather soon, tracing the old breweries becomes an interesting problem for collectors. Small brewers are still going out of business at a rapid rate. The few large brewers who advertise and distribute nationally have made the survival of small local breweries very difficult.

The story of the beer industry in America can be told through a study of the hundreds of different embossments on nineteenth-century bottles. Few of the names are familiar today and the bottles are the only monument to a small business enterprise that is quickly disappearing. It is likely that "local brew" will soon be a thing of the past.

The collateral material available for the beer bottle collector is extensive. Advertising trays are, perhaps, the most desired. These colorful pictorial trays were made for distribution to bars and restaurants where a particular brand of beer was sold. Sometimes the companies who made the trays had special designs for a particular brewery. More often, stock trays with pictorial designs were used and a space left for printed advertising. Beer mugs with advertising of the nineteenth- and early twentieth-century breweries are still to be found as well as other advertising objects such as calendars, bar taps, ashtrays, early paper labels, and bar signs. Any examples of the advertising items distributed in the thirsty pre-Prohibition days of American history add interest and color to a growing and fascinating section of bottle collecting.

Chapter 16

MINERAL WATER, CARBONATED WATER, AND SOFT DRINK BOTTLES

THE curative powers of carbonated waters and mineral springs were a prerogative of the wealthy in eighteenth-century Europe. Wealthy Americans were to ape this fashion in the nineteenth century. In Europe, "rest cures" at famous watering hotels were not only fashionable, but were thought to cure any ill. Luxury hotels sprang up wherever there were springs bubbling forth gaseous waters from the earth. Enormous amounts of money were spent to establish vacation spots where one could have cured any ailment from "chronic catarrh of the nose" to "gout, obesity or diabetes."

Where the springs bubbled forth their muddy waters shrines were built, and in order to keep the clients happy while they were becoming healthy, garden parties, symphonic concerts, fireworks, flower fetes, and great balls were given frequently. Doctors and nurses were on hand day and night to supervise the "cures" and listen to complaints.

One luxurious mineral springs resort in Franzenbad, Czechoslovakia, advertised "two big springs gushing

LEFT: *Middletown Healing Springs, Grays & Clark, Middletown, Vt. Dark amber. H. 9¼ in.* Rebner

RIGHT: *Gettysburg Katalysine Water. Dark olive-green. H. 9¾ in.* Rebner

forth by the impetus of their own carbonic acid from a depth of 30 m. to a height of 10 m." and an "inhalatorium of the springs with up-to-date cells and public halls for inhalation." Spas all over Europe vied with each other for the opportunity of curing all the ills of the rich. These spas enjoyed periods of enormous prosperity from the late eighteenth century through the beginning of this century.

It took only until a wealthy upper class developed in America that mineral spring resorts became popular. The most famous spa, of course, was Saratoga Springs in Saratoga County, New York. The springs were first discovered in the eighteenth century and water from Saratoga was bottled and sold as early as 1820. A summer resort with hotels built in grand style in the manner of the European spas developed around the springs. The addition of a race track in the 1850s attracted healthy clients and kept the ailing from becoming too bored. People took the waters while recuperating from busy social seasons in the city and went to concerts, dances, and the races.

The rich, however, were not privileged in being the only people who could take advantage of the remarkable curative powers of Saratoga water. By the 1850s the water was being distributed all over America and some was even exported.

The early Saratoga mineral water bottles that are sought by collectors are dark green or amber and were made by the Mount Vernon Glass Works which moved from Oneida County to Saratoga County to supply bottles for Saratoga Springs. The earliest bottles date from 1844 and are heavy and squat with long necks and embossed lettering. There were, eventually, at least forty different brands of Saratoga Water distributed, and collectors search for bottles representing specimens of the different brands. Unusual colors or shades of color and a variation of sizes or shapes in the bottles are also sought.

Because the product itself cost little or nothing, the bottler's only appreciable expense was the bottling, distribution, and advertising. A great deal of money was spent extolling the curative powers of all bottled mineral

Geyser Springs, Saratoga Springs, N. Y. Dark olive-green. H. 9¾ in. Rebner

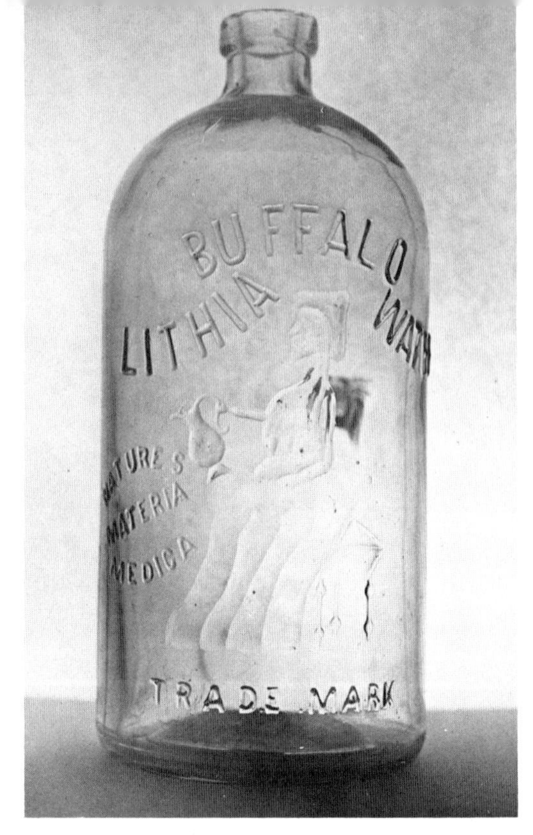

TOP LEFT: *Hathorn Springs, Saratoga, N. Y. H. 7¼ in.*
Rebner

RIGHT: *Buffalo Lithia Water, Nature's Materia Medica, Trade Mark. Aqua. H. 10 in.*
Rebner

BOTTOM: *W. & I. D. Clinton, Woodbridge, Conn., Premium Soda Water. Dark green. Blob-top bottle.*
Rebner

Clear embossed citrate of magnesia bottle with porcelain Lightning closure. H. 8¼. Mattatuck

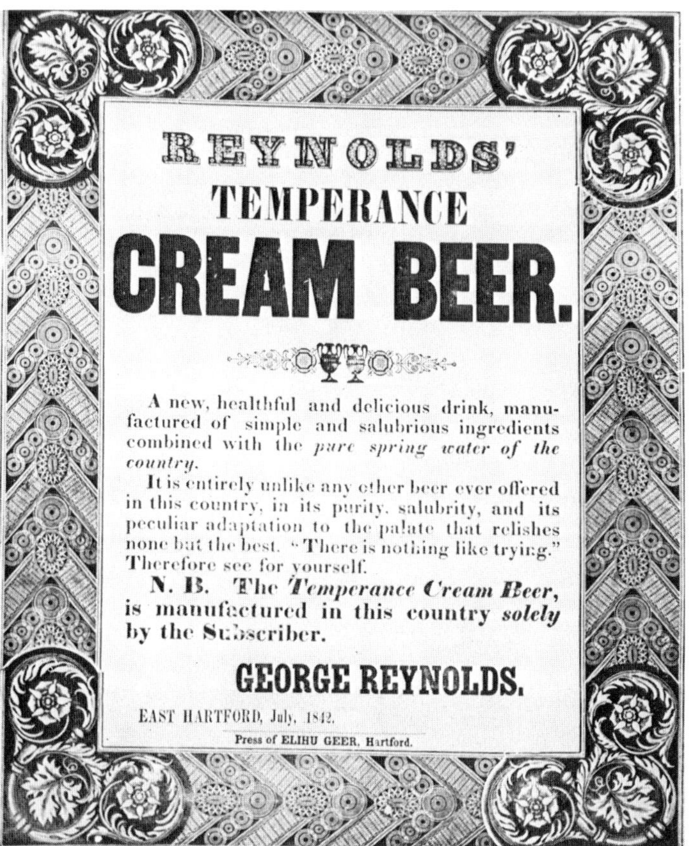

REYNOLDS'
TEMPERANCE
CREAM BEER.

A new, healthful and delicious drink, manufactured of simple and salubrious ingredients combined with the *pure spring water of the country*.

It is entirely unlike any other beer ever offered in this country, in its purity, salubrity, and its peculiar adaptation to the palate that relishes none but the best. "There is nothing like trying." Therefore see for yourself.

N. B. The *Temperance Cream Beer*, is manufactured in this country *solely* by the Subscriber.

GEORGE REYNOLDS.

EAST HARTFORD, July, 1842.

Press of ELIHU GEER, Hartford.

ABOVE: *Carbonated water was sold as a mild medication at first. This brand was supposed to cure rheumatism and gout. Dark green turn-mold bottle, corked. Kick-up base. H. 11½ in.* Mattatuck

LEFT: *Advertising broadside dated 1842.* Mattatuck

RIGHT: *Directions for making carbonated drinks from 1825 "receipt" book.*

Seltzer water.

Take of water any quantity. Impregnate it witl about ten times its volume of carbonic acid gas, b means of a forcing pump.

Liquid Magnesia.

Take of water, 1 gallon, carbonate of magnesia 3 drachms, and impregnate it as above.

Potass water.

Take one ounce of subcarbonate of potass, an impregnate as above.

Soda water.

Take 2 ounces of subcarbonate of soda, and im pregnate as above.

BELOW: *Sarsaparilla soda powders to be mixed with water. Clear glass. H. 10 in.*

Mattauck

water and, in the case of Saratoga, promoting the hotels and the town. These early advertisements are of interest to bottle collectors as collateral material. Hotel brochures, artfully designed and executed, are not too difficult to find since many of them were "too pretty to throw away." Souvenirs of the great spas are also interesting as related material, as are things from many of the hotels that have been torn down.

While mineral waters are a natural product, artificially carbonated water is an eighteenth-century invention attributed to Dr. Joseph Priestly, who came to this country in 1794 and was a close friend of Thomas Jefferson. Priestly was an English chemist and clergyman who suffered persecution in his own country. Although scientists had been attempting to learn how to carbonate water for a long time, Priestly's method of carbonation was the first practical one.

Early records indicate that "sparkling water" was being marketed in this country at the beginning of the eighteenth century. Sold at first as a cure, soda fountains were opened in drugstores and confectioners, and small local bottling industries grew in areas where the population warranted them. In the 1830s John Matthews of New York invented a method of carbonating water by using marble chips. Matthews purchased all the scrap marble from the construction of St. Patrick's Cathedral (which was begun in 1858) and produced an enormous amount of soda with the marble chips.

There are various conflicting stories about the earliest attempts to flavor carbonated water. The first seems to have been by a Philadelphia pharmacist, Townsend Speakman, who added fruit juice to a carbonated medical concoction to mask the bitter taste. Eugene Roussel, also from Philadelphia and a perfume dealer, is said to have invented flavored soda in 1839. Whoever it was started an enormous industry that has kept American bottlers busy for over a hundred years. Flavored soda became the temperance drink during the late nineteenth century. No longer quite convinced of the curative powers of carbonated water, Americans began to drink

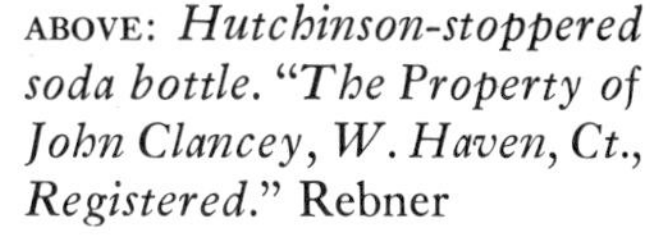
ABOVE: *Hutchinson-stoppered soda bottle. "The Property of John Clancey, W. Haven, Ct., Registered."* Rebner

LEFT: *Three Hutchinson-stoppered bottles. Light aqua. Left: Immels, Reading, Pa. H. 6½ in. Center: Bottling Co., Concord, N. H. Right: Otto Brandt, Newark, N. J. "This Bottle not to be Sold." All three were made c. 1900.* Rebner

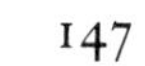

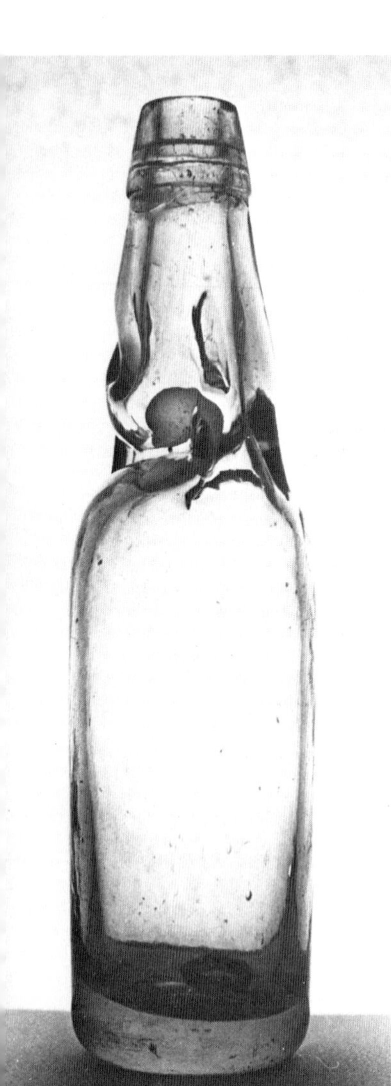

soda to quench what appears to be an unassuageable thirst.

Toward the beginning of this century small local firms bottled beverages that had limited distribution until, finally, as improved transportation made wider distribution possible, some of these small firms grew larger. After 1900 names like Moxie, Coca-Cola, Hires Root Beer and Pepsi-Cola became household words.

The success story of Coca-Cola is, in a way, a history of the change from the touting of carbonated beverages as a kind of mild medication to a pleasurable, seemingly harmless, drink. Coca-Cola syrup was first sold at a fountain as a headache cure and it was the accidental addition of the syrup to carbonated water that led to the drink that is world famous today. Dr. John S. Pemberton, a druggist in Atlanta, Georgia, discovered the formula for the syrup while experimenting with French wine coca, a medicine for headaches.

The first bottles used for Coca-Cola were plain, unembossed Hutchinson-type bottles and were probably secondhand. The earliest embossed bottles are marked by Joseph A. Biederharn of Vicksburg, Mississippi. Mr. Biederharn missed what later turned out to be a very good business enterprise by not bottling a large amount of Coca-Cola. In 1899 two lawyers from Chattanooga, Benjamin Franklin Thomas and Joseph Brown Whitehead, purchased the bottling rights to Coca-Cola for a token dollar. At the time Coca-Cola was thought of as a soda fountain drink and the company was interested in selling only the syrup.

Franchised bottling plants sprang up quickly in many cities. Bottles with the embossments of individual bottling companies were made. By 1916, the familiar Coca-Cola bottle had been designed and was the standard bottle for all Coca-Cola sold. It was invented by two employees of the Root Glass Company in Terre Haute, Indiana, and it has been said that the shape was inspired by a drawing of a cola nut. The distinctive shape, thought by many designers to be a perfectly designed package, has been called the "Mae West" or "Hobble Skirt" bottle.

OPPOSITE PAGE

TOP: *Unembossed round-bottom mineral water bottle. Aqua. These bottles cannot be stood on end. H. 9 in. c. 1880.* Rebner

BOTTOM: *Codd marble-stoppered bottle, sometimes called "pig" bottle, was filled upside down. A rubber ring that fitted inside the neck formed a closure with the marble which was held in place by the pressure of the gas in the soda. Aqua. H. 9 in.* Rebner

THIS PAGE

BELOW: *Embossed round-bottom soda bottle. Bolen & Byrne, New York, Aerated Beverages. Aqua. H. 9 in.* Rebner

ABOVE RIGHT: *Embossed soda bottle. Blob-top. "This Bottle not to be Sold." Other side has embossment for Borchardt and Batrz, Waterbury, Conn. in circle. Aqua. H. 7½ in.* Rebner

LEFT: *Embossed soda bottle with Lightning stopper. Aqua. H. 9 in.* Rebner

BELOW: *Embossed soda bottle. Clear glass. Blob-top. H. 9 in.* Hardy

ABOVE LEFT: *Soda bottle embossed "Nu-Grape, a flavor you can't forget. Pat. applied for March 9, 1920." Light aqua. H. 7¾ in.* Rebner

RIGHT: *Embossed bottle in clear glass. "Soda water, 6 fluid ounces, Property of Coca Cola Bottling Co., Lima, Ohio."* Rebner

BELOW: *Newspaper advertisement for confectioner who sold soda and mineral water. Note date in Dentist's ad. below.* Mattatuck

MEIGS & TROTT,

No. 74 EAST MAIN STREET, ICE CREAM, plain and in forms. Water Ices, Charlottede Russe, made to order. Soda and Mineral Waters, Ottawa Beer, Confectioneries, our own make. Plain and Fancy Ornamented Cakes. Wheat, Rye, Graham and Aerated Bread, Rusk, Rolls, Pies, etc., etc. Crackers sold to the trade. Parties and picnics supplied at short notice.

G. H. WATERS, DENTIST.

☞ Dental Rooms Opened Oct. 1, 1852. ☜

This office is especially noted for its nicely fitting and well adjusted Artificial Teeth, as also the careful and thorough manner in which all operations

LEFT: *Soda bottle, embossed "Casco - Coca - Cola Bottling Works, Bottle pat'd. Dec. 29, 1925, Portland, Me." Aqua. H. 7¾ in.* Rebner

RIGHT: *Bottle embossed "Coca Cola Bottling Co., Waterbury, Conn., Registered." Aqua. H. 7½ in.* Rebner

BELOW: *Coca-Cola 2¢ returnable bottle. Aqua. H. 7¾ in.* Rebner

Until about forty years ago, almost all Coca-Cola bottles had the name of the bottler and his location embossed on the bottom, and these labeled bottles have become collector's items. Billions of those bottles were made and bottling plants from all over the world were represented. Since the bottles were returnable, many were taken to other places and bottles from almost anywhere can be found in any particular location.

Coca-Cola bottle collectors look for the earliest bottles and a variety of embossments. Interesting bottle shapes made before the famous pinched-waist bottle in unusual colors make up the most prized specimens.

From its beginning the Coca-Cola Company has spent an unusual proportion of its earnings on advertising. Trays, glasses, mugs, thermometers shaped like Coke bottles, jewelry, cigarette lighters, miniature bottles, and many other items have all been used as promotion and all are now in demand by collectors. Currently, even the 2¢ returnable bottles that have been replaced by the "no deposit, no return" bottles are being put aside by knowl-

TOP: *Hires Root Beer mug, mocha glaze. Child holding identical mug with his picture on it.* Author

BELOW: *Hires Root Beer mug, white ironstone. "Hires" in red letters on reverse side.* Author

Majolica mug, tan and cobalt, for Dr. Swett's Original Root Beer. False bottom halfway from base of mug. H. 6 in. c. 1900. Calabrese

edgeable dealers and collectors. What started a few years ago as an amusing hobby thought to be somewhat "camp" now interests serious collectors who, perhaps, see the Coca-Cola bottle as a symbol as familiar as the American flag.

Embossed soda pop bottles of local interest comprise other collections. Early bottles with rounded bottoms, bottles with closures made before the crown cap, and bottles of any unusual color, bottles with interesting embossments, are all looked for today. The history of the soft drink business in America is recent enough for collectors to find a wide selection of bottles and related material for a relatively small investment.

Chapter 17

INK BOTTLES

A GREAT deal of preparation was required before an eighteenth-century gentleman could "take pen in hand" to write a letter. Ink, an expensive commodity when purchased, was usually homemade from a myriad of available "receipts." The feather quill, the only pen used then, had to be carefully chosen and carved to a fine point which too quickly became dull. Sand and sealing wax had to be close at hand also. Writing with a quill pen required constant arm movement from the paper to the ink bottle and the act of writing was slow and laborious.

One cannot collect ink bottles without knowing something of the history of the development of writing implements in America. The feather quill was not replaced by the metal nib until the middle of the nineteenth century. It was not until late in the century that fountain pens were manufactured and in general use, although they were invented in 1830. The changes in the types of writing implements in use had a direct bearing on the styles of ink containers made at a particular period.

INKS, &c.

A fine black ink, for common purposes and for the copying press.

Put Aleppo galls, well bruised, 4½ oz. and logwood chipped, 1 oz. with 3 pints soft water, into a stoneware mug: slowly boil, until one quart remains: add, well powdered, the pure green crystals of sulphate of iron, 2½ oz. blue vitriol or verdigris, (I think the latter better,) ½ oz. gum arabic, 2 oz. and brown sugar, 2 oz. Shake it occasionally a week after making: then after standing a day, decant and cork. To prevent moulding add a little brandy or alcohol.

Z

The common copperas will not answer so well, as it has already absorbed oxygen.

To make common black ink.

Pour a gallon of boiling soft water on a pound of powdered galls, previously put into a proper vessel. Stop the mouth of the vessel, and set it in the sun in summer, or in winter where it may be warmed by any fire, and let it stand two or three days. Then add half a pound of green vitriol powdered, and having stirred the mixture well together with a wooden spatula, let it stand again for two or three days, repeating the stirring, when

The earliest containers for commercially made ink were pottery bottles which were imported from England. Decorative inkwells in many shapes and styles graced the desks of our more affluent and literate citizens. Inkwells, in decorative stands, were made by the great pottery, porcelain, and glass manufacturers of Europe. Since ink bottles and inkwells are so closely allied and in some cases are the same thing, it would be difficult to discuss one without the other.

One type of inkwell that was extremely popular was invented by Josiah Wedgwood in the 1770s. This inkwell was innovative in that it was designed to keep the ink in the pen well at a constant level so that the writer's fingers would not become inkstained. The Wedgwood inkwell, first made in engine-turned basalt, was the most practical design of any subsequent inkwells made. It was sold with instructions as to how it should be filled, since it worked on the vacuum principle. The Wedgwood firm alone made so many different styles and types of inkwells,

Directions for making ink printed in 1825. Watkins

many of which were imported to America, that a collector could specialize in these only.

The collector of American bottles, however, is more interested in the small inks, made by the early glass houses, than in the contemporary decorative wells that were imported. All of the early glass houses seem to have made the small containers for ink that were used on the writing table. Master ink bottles in pint and quart size from which the small bottles were filled do not seem to be as plentiful.

Inkwells, ink bottles and master inks have become popular bottles to collect in recent years. The earliest small bottles and inkwells, of blown-in-mold glass with pontil scars, are now scarce and difficult to find. As is true of other early American glass, those ink bottles and inkwells in the least common colors command the highest prices. Those that can be attributed to a particular glass house are in greatest demand.

Besides the truly antique inkwells and bottles, all bottles for ink made up to 1900 are eagerly sought by col-

LEFT: *Rare inkwell. Dark olive amber. "J. P. F." was J. P. Foster who was superintendent of the Pitkin Glass Works, Manchester, Conn., after 1810. H. 1⅝ in. W. 2½ in.* Mattatuck

RIGHT: *Ink bottle, light golden amber. Possibly Stoddard, New Hampshire. Early nineteenth century. H. 2 in.* Rebner

RIGHT: *Inkwell, made in England. Ground pontil. H. 2¾ in. c. 1860.* Hardy

BELOW: *Turtle-shape ink bottle embossed "J. & I. E. M." Aqua.* Hardy

BELOW: *Group of ink bottles. From left to right: Turtle shape embossed "J. M. for J. and I. E. Moore, Warren, Massachusetts." Aqua. H. 1½ in.; Embossed "J. & I. E. M.," cobalt blue; Six-sided conical ink, cobalt; Eight-sided conical (also called "umbrella" shape) ink in aqua.* Rebner

lectors and there are many from which to choose. Over a thousand different bottles have been catalogued and probably there are many more yet to be found and identified. The earlier bottles, those meant to be used with a quill or nib, are most interesting and attractive. When the fountain pen came into common use, the ink bottle from which it was filled could be kept out of sight in a drawer and as a result, the design of the later bottles became somewhat standardized.

Ink bottles were made in many interesting shapes in the nineteenth century and collectors look for the most unusual ones. Obviously, good design requires that an ink bottle should not tip easily, so that a common early shape is the umbrella or conical inkwell. The side-spouted shape, the dome shape, the igloo and boat shapes were all popular and were made in a variety of colors. All old inks are short, squat, and bottom-heavy for obvious practical reasons.

Collectors of bottles with embossed lettering find that there are many ink bottles to choose from. Master inks as

Ink bottle embossed with patent date. Aqua. Rebner

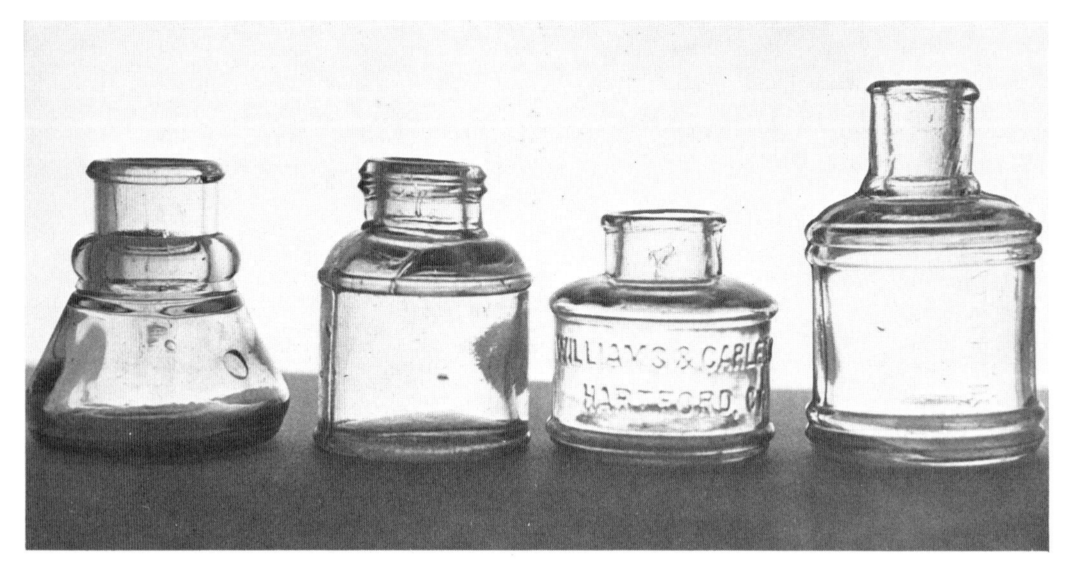

TOP: *Three ink bottles in round, conical, and square shapes. From left to right: cobalt; green glass; clear glass.* Rebner

CENTER: *Group of ink bottles, two with embossments. All light aqua.* Rebner

BOTTOM: *Bottle for Caw's ink. Aqua. H. 2¼ in.* Rebner

LEFT: *"Harrison's Columbian Ink." Twelve-panelled bottle is aqua and was made at the Whitney Glass Works. H. 6 in.* Rebner

BELOW: *Cobalt blue ink bottle. Six-sided.* Rebner

BELOW: *Group of labeled ink bottles for Carter's, Higgins and Stafford's ink.* Rebner

RIGHT: *Pottery master ink bottles. From left to right: J. Bourne & Son, Patentees, Denby Pottery near Denby; P. & J. Arnold, London.*

BELOW: *Labeled J. & I. E. Moore ink bottle in "house" shape. H. 2⅞ in.* Rebner

well as the small inks were made with the names of the firms embossed. This of course makes identification easier.

One of the advantages in limiting one's collection of old bottles to inks is, of course, the infinite variety of old glass that is represented in a comprehensive collection. For people with limited space a large variety of inks in many shapes and colors can be displayed in a small area. Because of their small size and the fact that ink bottles were made sturdily to begin with, large numbers of these small bottles have survived intact and bottle diggers are frequently rewarded by finding ink bottles that are in perfect condition.

Many of the same firms that made and bottled ink in the late nineteenth century also made other products such as shoe blacking and hair dye, and these were sold in the same kind of bottle. The small bottles that are called "inks" did not always contain writing fluid. Labels or remnants of labels that might still be left on an ink bottle are important and help positive identification.

Along with old ink bottles and inkwells, other material

TOP LEFT: *Carter's master ink bottle in aqua with double collared lip. H. 7½ in.* Rebner

RIGHT: *Sanford's master ink bottle. Screw-thread closure. Aqua. 9¼ in.* Rebner

BOTTOM: *Master ink embossed "S. Staffords inks/Made in U. S. A./This bottle contains one full quart." Cobalt blue. H. 7 in.* Rebner

that has to do with writing is interesting. Quills and metal pen points, desk accessories such as stamp boxes, sand holders, wax seals, directions for making ink, and early fountain pens are all collateral material. Early advertisements and catalogs of firms that made the bottles can be collected also, and they will help identify ink bottles.

In these days of the disposable ballpoint pen, it is easy to understand why, in the light of the effort once needed to write a letter, so much emphasis was put on the teaching of beautiful and legible penmanship. It is not unlikely that early examples of handwriting of the eighteenth and nineteenth centuries will soon be important collector's items. Meticulous penmanship seems to have become as rare as an eighteenth- or early nineteenth-century ink bottle.

ABOVE: *Traveling ink bottle, "Waterman's Ideal Ink," on spring-type cap.* Rebner

RIGHT: *Wood barrel-shaped traveling ink bottle. H. 2 in.* Rebner

Chapter 18

PERFUME, SCENT, AND COLOGNE BOTTLES

THE use of perfume dates back to the beginnings of civilization when strong scents were used in religious rites as well as for personal adornment. Until this century, when indoor plumbing became possible, perfume was used to "cover up one smell with another" and was a necessity rather than a luxury. The use of fragrances distilled from flowers, spices, fruit, and wood is as old as the history of glass.

Perfume has enjoyed many periods of great popularity, but there have been other times in history when it was frowned upon as being evil. In the relatively short period of American history there has never been a time when perfume of one sort or another was not used. Perfume flasks were made in large amounts by our earliest glass houses and these small jewel-like bottles are the most beautiful of all early American glass.

In the eighteenth century, perfume and scent were so important a part of one's dress that tiny bottles were made to be worn or carried on one's person like jewelry. Scent, which was stronger than perfume, had an added

PERFUMERY AND COSMETICS.

To make eau de Cologne.

Take of essence de bergamotte, 3 oz. neroli, 1½ drachms, cedrat, 2 do., lemon, 3 do., oil of rosemary, 1 do., spirit of wine, 12 lbs., spirit of rosemary, 3½ do., eau de melisse de Carmes, 2¼ do. Mix. Distil in balneum mariæ, and keep it in a cold cellar or icehouse for some time. It is used as a cosmetic, and made with sugar into a ratafia.

Eau de melisse de Carmes.

Take of dried balm leaves, 4 oz. dried lemon-peel, 2 do., nutmegs and coriander seeds, each, 1 oz. cloves, cinnamon, and dried angelica roots, each, 4 dr. spirit of wine, 2 lbs. brandy, 2 ditto. Steep and distil in balneum mariæ, re-distil, and keep for some time in a cold cellar.

Original receipt for the same.—Take of spirit of balm, 8 pints, lemon peel, 4 do., nutmegs and coriander seeds, each 2 do., rosemary, marjoram, thyme, hyssop, cinnamon, sage, aniseed, cloves, angelica roots, each 1 pint. Mix, distil and keep

ABOVE: *Directions, written near the beginning of the nineteenth century, for making cologne at home.*

LEFT: *Hand-painted milk glass jar for sachet musk powder. H. 4½ in. c. 1850.* Hardy

RIGHT: *Small bottle, pale aqua, pontilled. Old printed labels are glued to bottle. H. 2¼ in.* Mattatuck

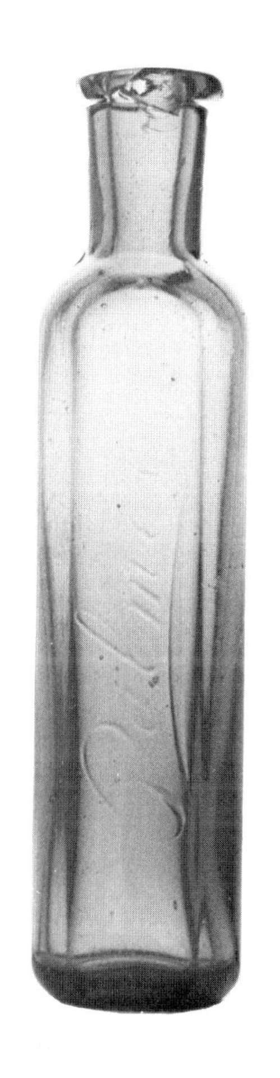

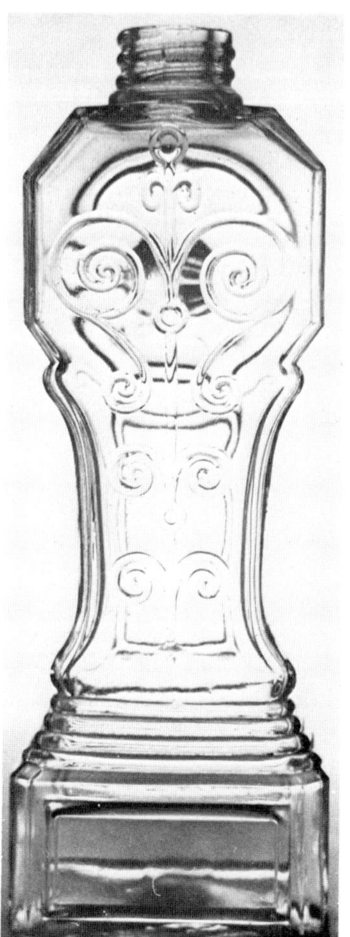

TOP LEFT: *Bottle embossed "Zhongiva" in script. Probably perfume bottle. H. 4½ in. c. 1870.* Rebner

RIGHT: *Emerald green bottle for Palmer perfume. H. 4¾ in.* Rebner

BOTTOM LEFT: *Embossed perfume or cologne bottle in shape of clock. H. 6 in.* Rebner

RIGHT: *White glass bottle embossed "C. W. Laird, Perfumer, Broadway, N. Y." H. 4½ in.* Rebner

RIGHT: *Lithographed trade card for "Lazell's Unrivalled Perfumes."* Mattatuck

BELOW: *Dresser bottles for perfume. From left to right: Light blue opalescent glass with gold bandings; Blue frosted glass with gold decorations.* Mattatuck

ingredient, ammonia, and it was used to revive the wearer from fainting spells. Perfume in larger bottles that often came in their own fitted cases went on journeys as a means of making the close quarters of carriages bearable. It was used for cleaning the dust of the road off one's skin as well as to cover odors.

Eighteenth-century perfume bottles made in America were much like their counterparts being made in Europe at the time. Free-blown or blown-in-mold bottles were made in a variety of patterns and colors. Cork stoppers were used. With the invention of the hinged mold at the beginning of the nineteenth century, decorative shapes and designs were made. It was not until the latter half of the nineteenth century in this country that perfume and scent began to be commercially manufactured, packaged, and distributed. By this time synthetic aromatic substances had been developed for the manufacture of perfume and other cosmetics. Cologne, which is perfume diluted with alcohol, was made and sold in large quantities in America around 1900. Because cologne was

LEFT: *Cobalt blue glass dresser bottle. Hand-decorated in yellow, gold, and white. H. 6 in.* Hardy

RIGHT: *Milk glass dresser bottle, hand painted. Pontil scar. H. 5½ in.* Mattatuck

LEFT: *Dresser bottle for cologne. Hand enameled wreaths and garlands in red and green. English. H. 6 in. c. 1820.* Hardy

RIGHT: *Dresser bottle for perfume or cologne. Amethyst shading to clear toward base. H. 5¼ in.* Hardy

BELOW: *Perfume or cologne dresser bottle. Applied foil label with hand-painted banners. H. 8 in.* Hardy

cheaper to make and could be sold in larger quantities for less money than perfume, it became popular right away. Cologne bottles are generally larger than perfume bottles.

Perfume has always been sold in elaborate packages with special care being given to the design and quality of the bottle. Perfume bottles, although commercial, have been designed and made by some of the greatest glass houses of the world and closely follow styles that are contemporary in the decorative arts. Because France has long been the world center for perfumes, there are French bottles signed by Lalique, Gallé, and other glass designers of the late nineteenth and early twentieth centuries. Victorian, Art Nouveau, and Art Deco bottles can be found, and there are many modern French bottles that are outstanding, since the custom of packaging perfume in superbly designed bottles continues today.

As is the case with the decorative whiskey bottles that are collected nowadays, one purchases the bottle when one buys perfume. The cost of highly decorative bottles is added into the total cost of the package and often the same brand will be offered in less elaborate bottles for those interested only in the product.

There have been hundreds of different designs for French perfume bottles made over the years with some brands using the same design for identification of their product and others changing their bottle designs often. For the collector there is probably no better value than French perfume bottles. They are not yet as expensive as many other bottles and they are usually of better quality glass. A great many figural bottles are available as well as those that reflect the decorative styles of the past.

French-made perfume bottles have been somewhat overlooked since most of the literature has emphasized American-made bottles. However, judging from the large amount of French perfume that has been purchased in this country, it should be obvious that a great many bottles are available and a collection of the more interesting ones can be gathered for very little investment at present. This is another interesting category for the collector whose funds and space are limited.

Trade card for "Florida Water." Mattatuck

TOP: *Clear glass perfume bottles with gold decoration on stopper and shoulders of bottles. Ebony box is brass inlaid with "odeurs" inlaid on top of lid.* Author

CENTER: *Etched glass perfume bottle (left) with cloisonné stopper. H. 3 in. Emerald green bottle (right) with silver overlay. H. 2¾ in. c. 1890.* Hardy

BOTTOM: *Hand enameled perfume bottle (left), gold cap in swirl design. H. 3 in. Etched glass perfume bottle (right) with pink cloisonné stopper. H. 2½ in.* Hardy

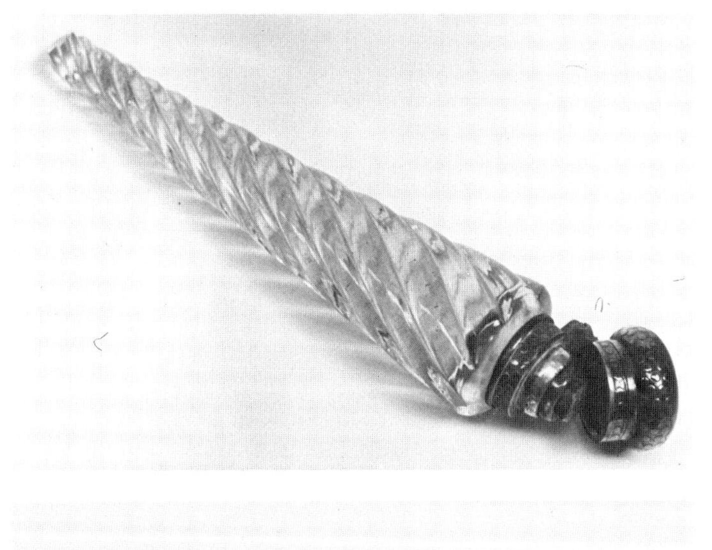

TOP: *Perfume flask for purse. Twisted ribbed pattern. Silver-gilt embossed cap. L. 4 in. c. 1850.* Mattatuck

CENTER: *Double perfume flask. Ruby glass, silver caps. Made in England. L. 6 in.* Hardy

BOTTOM: *Collection of overlay glass perfume pocket bottles. Smallest bottle on left is 1½ in. Colors are green, salmon pink, red, and blue.* Hardy

LEFT: *Wedgwood blue jasper perfume flask made to be worn on chain around neck. L. 2½ in. c. 1790.* Author

RIGHT: *Enameled glass perfume flask. Pink and gold predominating. Silver gilt cap. L. 6½ in.* Hardy

The collector of perfume bottles might also collect atomizers made for spraying perfume and cologne. These were not always commercial bottles but were made to be refilled and used on the dressing table. There were a great many atomizers made toward the end of the last century and the different colors, styles, and types of glass that are representative of the art glass period can be found. Dresser bottles for perfume representing the many decorative types of glass that have been made in America and abroad can be found. This type of bottle is expensive, but has the advantage of being of historic and artistic value.

Design for perfume flasks and bottles has historically taxed the imagination of glassmakers all over the world. Since perfume is the most expensive liquid that is bottled, it has deserved commensurately expensive and artistic containers. In the single area of small perfume flasks for milady's purse, there are hundreds of gem-like containers from which the collector may choose. Tiny bottles, made to hang from chatelaines worn by women in the late

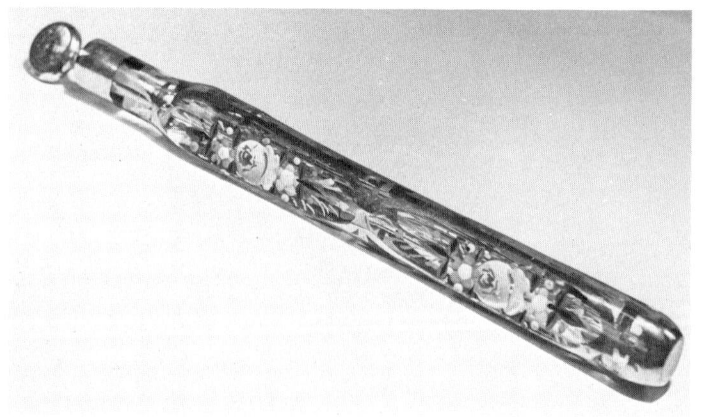

LEFT: *Frosted glass perfume bottle signed "Lalique." Made in France in style of early twentieth-century Art Deco.* Cross

RIGHT: *Aqua opaque glass with black overlay, this perfume atomizer is in typical Art Nouveau design.*

BELOW: *Child's cologne bottle with pink plastic cap. Made in Holland in figural of owl dressed in man's clothing. H. 3 in.*

seventeenth, eighteenth, and nineteenth centuries, represent every precious material and method for decorating that was known in those centuries. Silver, gold and semiprecious stones were made into tiny bottles for scent. Josiah Wedgwood made magnificent jasper bottles to be worn in this manner.

Within the specialty of collecting perfume bottles, one may specialize further in pocket scent bottles, cologne bottles, commercial bottles or dresser bottles. As we shall see later, there are many collectors today who specialize in the toy-like bottles of the Avon Company and because of the myriad of bottles available here, even Avon collectors specialize in particular types of bottles made by this company.

Some collectors look for only the decorative bottles that were sold empty, while others search only for the commercial bottles. In the former, one might specialize in only one type. For instance, people collect Wedgwood perfume flasks or colorful glass overlay flasks.

Collateral material such as the tiny sample bottles of

perfume are now in demand as well as early advertisements for some of the noted perfumes and colognes. From the largest cologne bottles to the smallest scent bottle, the story of perfume packaging is fascinating and can lead to most interesting collections.

ABOVE: *Perfume bottles from 1920s advertisements. Designed in Art Deco style, these bottles are now very collectible.*

RIGHT: *New perfume bottle that will become important collector's item. Stopper has frosted glass peace dove in flight. Designed and made by Lalique-Nina Ricci "L'Air du Temps" perfume.*

Chapter 19

BARBER BOTTLES

THE local barber shop was the social club of the late nineteenth century. Men met in congenial surroundings safe from the feminine eye and leisurely read the *Police Gazette* and exchanged local gossip. An indication of success in small town life was the sight of one's own shaving cup on display at the barber shop along with those of other noted citizens.

Local barbers made or bought in bulk their own restoratives and tonics for the hair and these liquids were poured into fancy barber bottles that decorated the shelf in front of the mirror. These bottles were decorative and many were printed or hand-painted. Similar bottles for the dresser were sold for home use as well.

The manufacture of decorative barber bottles took place during a period of American glass making when experiments in different and unusual techniques for producing and decorating glass were being made, such as in new colors and textures as well as patterns for glass; and ancient techniques were also copied. From about 1880 to the first decade of this century a great deal of mag-

nificent and interesting pieces of decorative glass were produced. In this country and abroad designers and decorators such as Louis Comfort Tiffany and Emile Gallé studied the properties of ancient glass and produced many varied kinds of decorative pieces of glass that were adapted from it. Opaque colored glass, iridescent glass, overlay glass, and many other unique and beautiful types were made. For those interested in decorative rather than commercial bottles, barber bottles are an interesting category in which to specialize. Barber bottles can also be found in the styles of the Sandwich Glass House. Popular types of glass, from the late Victorian to the many Art Nouveau styles, can be found in this category.

Most barbers owned sets of barber stand bottles. Preferred and steady customers had their names printed in gold under the legends "bay rum" or "witch hazel." These personalized bottles are difficult to find and are highly prized by collectors of barber shop *memorabilia.* Many of these bottles had color lithographs of popular actresses or romantic scenes which had been pasted to

LEFT: *Pair of barber bottles in yellow opaque enameled glass. H. 8¼ in.* Rebner

RIGHT: *Enameled glass, hand-lettered in black. Barber bottle for witch hazel. H. 8 in.* Rebner

the bottle under a fitted panel of glass. Usually the name of the patron was printed in gold. The invention of the safety razor in 1903 caused the daily visit to the barber shop to come to an end for most men, and after that time the bottles were not made.

As well as Art Nouveau styles in American glass, Bohemian glass and other colored glass bottles for the barber shop were imported from Europe. Cut and pressed glass was also used and it was not uncommon for the fancier "tonsorial parlors" to feature matching personalized sets of bottle, shaving bowl, and pomade jar for their patrons.

The collector who is interested in decorative glass often has a difficult search when looking for barber bottles. Most of the better ones are in private collections and a great many were thrown out when no longer needed. Recent interest in Art Nouveau glass has caused the barber bottles attributed to the more important glassmakers of the period to become very scarce and expensive.

Collectors of barber bottles, often caught up in the nos-

Pattern glass barber bottle. H. 9 in. Rebner

RIGHT: *Personalized ironstone shaving mug of type kept at barber shop for regular customers.* Mattatuck

BELOW: *White glass talcum container from barber shop. Brass perforated screw cap. H. 5 in. c. 1890.* Palmieri

talgia for barber shop *memorabilia*, look for any related items from shaving mugs to barber poles. Advertising signs, barber chairs, and even straight razors and razor strops are currently being bought for collections.

Milk glass, satin glass, pressed or cut glass, silver overlay, and all the other magnificent types of glass made during the late nineteenth century in America or abroad can all be represented in a collection of barber bottles, providing the collector has the patience and the means. While undoubtedly one of the more expensive categories of bottle collecting, barber bottles are a safe investment and can be expected to increase in value.

Chapter 20

POTTERY BOTTLES AND JUGS

WHILE the majority of bottles dating from the eighteenth and nineteenth centuries were made of glass, a great many pottery bottles and jugs were produced also. Leather and metal were also used to make early containers for liquid. The use of pottery for bottles and jugs dates far back in civilization. However, our concern here is to place in age and category some of the bottles and jugs made of ceramics that were produced during the same years as most of the collectible glass bottles that we find today, and to examine the importance of including pottery bottles in a collection.

In certain categories it is almost impossible, if one is to have a truly representative collection, to avoid acquiring some pottery. The first master ink bottles, for instance, to be used in this country were made of pottery in England. Rum, gin, beer, and other alcoholic beverages were bottled in jugs and bottles made of pottery, and some of the most interesting and attractive figural decanters of nineteenth-century American manufacture were produced in Bennington, Vermont.

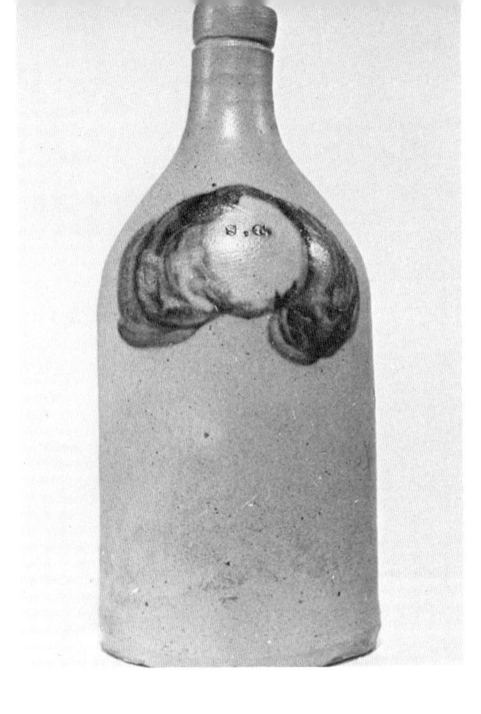

LEFT: *Pottery bottle. Light gray glaze. Blue underglaze decoration with impressed and painted initials, "S. G." H. 10¼ in.* Hardy

RIGHT: *Pottery bottle for beer or ale. H. 9¼ in. c. 1850.* Mattatuck

The greatest number of pottery bottles made to hold special products and found in America today came from England. By the end of the eighteenth century the ceramics industry was well established in the Staffordshire region of England to the point that before and after the Revolution American potters could not compete successfully. The American ceramics industry has never reached the heights of attainment of the glass industry. Just as we depended upon England for pottery before the Revolution, we continued to purchase a great deal of her pottery abroad after the War.

Although many small domestic potters turned out the essential jugs and bottles needed for storing and transporting liquids at the beginning of the nineteenth century, they were unable to make the finished vessels that were the products of generations of highly skilled potters of England. Just about all American-made pottery bottles and jugs found today are of the post-Revolutionary War period and many are much later than we might like to think. Rather crude jugs and bottles (but mostly jugs) were still being produced in this country at the beginning of this century and unless a jug is dated or can otherwise be traced, there is no way to tell when it was made.

Ceramic bottles can be divided into two major categories. The first is commercial bottles which were made to hold a particular product and which may or may not have advertising written on them. The second category includes all decorative and useful bottles; these were usually, but not always, sold empty. From the viewpoint of most bottle collectors, the first category is more interesting, since they are as concerned with the product that a container held as with the bottle itself. A great many bottles and jugs made of clay contain advertising that is incised or written in slip on or under the glaze. Most of the bottles and jugs of this type date from the latter half of the nineteenth century, but some are earlier. Pottery bottles or jugs with primitive decoration in slip or the name of the potter or the customer for whom the pot was made are of interest to the collector. Another method of identifying the product on ceramic bottles is by stamp-

LEFT: *Pottery jug, blue slip decoration. Brown glaze. H. 10 in. c. 1830.* Mattatuck

RIGHT: *Pottery jug of type made throughout last century. H. 10 in.* Author

ing the clay or printing the customers' names over or under the glaze.

Nineteenth-century English ginger beer bottles are collected by people interested in the history of the soft drink industry. The aforementioned British ink bottles and medicine bottles can be found in pottery and are important to those collectors who wish to have a comprehensive representation of all bottles made for a specific purpose. The earliest containers for preserving food at home were made of pottery and these would be an important part of a fruit jar collection. Mineral water bottles were made of clay, also, and brought to this country from Germany or Holland to satisfy the immigrants who wanted the water that they had been used to at home. Some drug bottles and jars for commercial products have been made and since the ceramics student has little interest in commercial pottery, it is up to the bottle collector to find and categorize these containers. Since many of the early containers made of glass and pottery had paper wrappers or labels, it is sometimes difficult to discover the original purpose for which the containers were made.

Historically, fine pottery and porcelain have been

LEFT: *Bennington book flask. "Traveler's Companion" impressed on spine. Brown and cream mottled glaze. H. 6¾ in. c. 1850.* Mattatuck

RIGHT: *Bennington flask with tavern scene framed by raspberries and vines. Pint.* Mattatuck

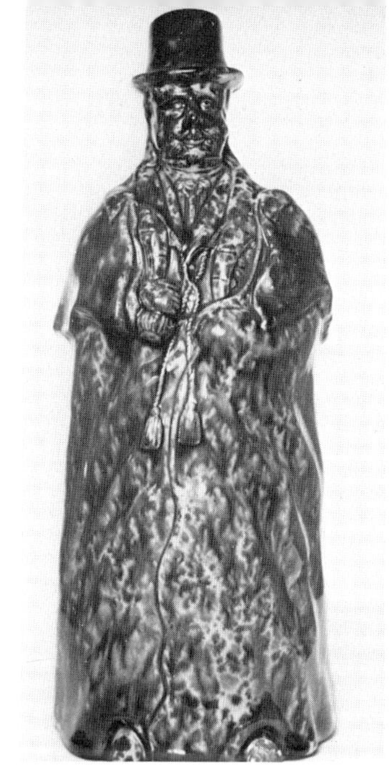

LEFT: *Bennington coachman bottle in Rockingham glaze. H. 10½ in.* Mattatuck

RIGHT: *Bennington coachman bottle in flint enamel glaze. H. 10½ in.* Mattatuck

BELOW: *Pottery bottle for soda or beer with Lightning stopper of porcelain. H. 11 in.* Rebner

made to order for distillers and there are many outstanding gift decanters of this type for collectors. Most of those that can be found date from the beginning of this century. Many of these bottles were made for scotch whiskey distillers and some of the great names of the British ceramics industry can be found on their bottoms. Although decorative in nature, they were originally made to hold a commercial product and many carry the stamp of the distiller on the bottom.

Two bottles of this type were made by Josiah Wedgwood at the beginning of this century and these should be of special interest to collectors of decorative commercial spirits bottles since there have been few times in the history of Wedgwood that they have made commercial bottles. Made in two types of ceramics, creamware and the more familiar jasper ware, both of these bottles have long been collector's items for the Wedgwood enthusiast. Made for Humphrey Taylor & Co., London; and bearing the stamp of this firm on the bottom, the Wedgwood bottles also bear the familiar impressed mark of the great Staffordshire potter. The jasper ware bottle is a soft green

color and has applied white classical bas-relief. The closure is a ceramic knob with an attached screw that holds a cork in place.

Commercial bottles of high quality were made by other Staffordshire potters for various whiskey firms and these include figural spirit flasks of the early nineteenth century. These were made of saltglaze stoneware and issued at the time of Reform agitation. Unfortunately, little attention has been given to the history of British commercial bottles and it will probably be up to American bottle collectors to fill this gap.

As for the decorative ceramic flasks and bottles made in America during the nineteenth century, perhaps the most outstanding were the figural bottles made at Bennington, Vermont. Bennington pottery bottles, particularly the flint enamel and Rockingham glaze pieces, are among the few successes of American ceramics of the nineteenth century. Although British prototypes of many of the shapes and glazes can be found, the quality and design of Bennington figural bottles are such that they have long been collected by American pottery enthusiasts. However, many Bennington bottles were made and they can still be found for sale at antique shops.

Bennington's figural bottles, in the familiar brown Rockingham glaze or the more desirable speckled flint enamel glazes, were made in the shape of books in several sizes, the familiar coachmen, and flasks embossed with a tavern scene. The Bennington pottery was established in the mid-1840s by Christopher Weber Fenton; the name of his firm was Lyman, Fenton & Company. The earlier bottles are marked "Fenton's Works/Bennington/Vermont." Between 1850 and 1858 the firm's name was changed to United States Pottery.

There are hundreds of other types of non-commercial bottles that have been made from ceramics rather than

Vinegar jug with label. Art Nouveau style of label indicates jug was probably made at turn of century. Mattatuck glass. Perfume flasks, for instance, were being made in England long before American glassmakers began to produce them. Wedgwood made many tiny flasks in jasper ware in the eighteenth century. Pratt and Wedgwood both made pots to hold products that were exported to America. Many of these pots had printed scenes in color on the lids.

The products that were packaged in ceramic jars or bottles that people now collect are French mustard, Chinese ginger, British and German beer, mineral water, Japanese sake, and various brands of whiskey. Marked pottery bottles or jugs, or those that can be properly identified as having been made to hold a particular product used in the past, all interest the bottle collector.

The use of pottery for decorative bottles in which whiskey is sold continues on a larger scale than ever before. Since most of these bottles have been made in the past ten years, this category of collecting will be discussed in a separate chapter. Today's bottle collector should be a student of ceramics as well as glass if he is going to invest in these new bottles to any extent. The ability to recognize successful design and execution in the area of ceramics should be important to the collector of old as well as new ceramic bottles.

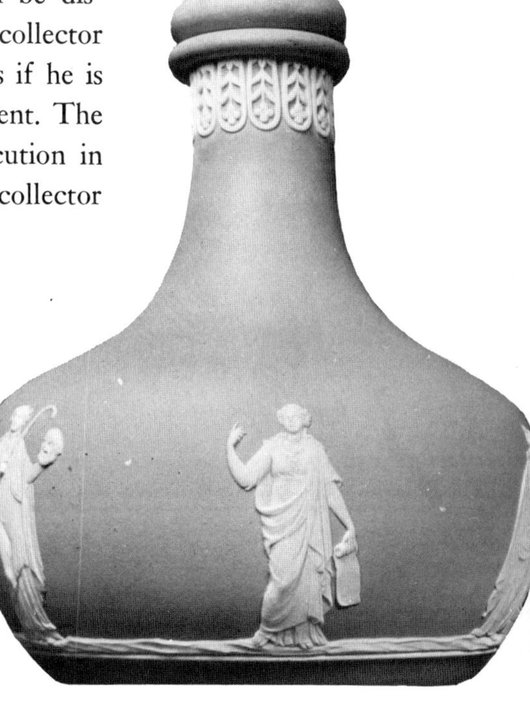

Green jasper bottle made by Wedgwood for Humphrey, Taylor & Co., London. Its white bas relief is of rather good quality for a commercial bottle. Mark on bottom of decanter is shown at left. Author

RIGHT: *Advertisement for Mason jars from 1880 newspaper.* Mattatuck

BELOW: *Early preserve or food jar. Pale aqua. H. 7⅛ in. c. 1850.* Mattatuck

s25da wtf

Fruit Jars.

MASON'S FRUIT JARS,

GLASS TOP JELLY GLASSES,

TIN TOP JELLY GLASSES,

COMMON JELLY GLASSES,

AT LOW PRICES AT THE

Big Pitcher Crockery Store

No 2 Irving Block,

G. R. HALLAS.

mr1dawtf

BELOW: *Table of fruit jars showing variety of closures that were used in the late nineteenth century.*

Chapter 21

MILK BOTTLES, FRUIT JARS, AND OTHER HOUSEHOLD BOTTLES

IT is difficult to believe that a phrase as common as "a bottle of milk" may soon disappear from the English language. Waxed cardboard containers and plastic cartons have made glass as a practical container for milk all but obsolete. For practical reasons dairies in America have all but phased out the glass milk bottle. Astute collectors realize that the milk bottle has had a very short history and have begun to collect the older, more interesting bottles. There will come a time when all glass milk bottles will be collectors' items and that time is not far away.

As was the case with beer bottles, milk was not sold in bottles until fairly late, brought about by the discovery of pasteurization and the resulting awareness that in order for disease to be avoided, food had to be sterile. The milk bottle has had a short fifty-year history and home milk deliveries will also become an unnecessary service we will shortly remember with nostalgia.

The problems of unclean milk plagued farmers and their customers throughout the nineteenth century.

Smalley "Full measure" quart fruit jar (left). Zinc screw type cover. Pat. Dec. 1892, April 17, 1896. Atlas "Strong Shoulder" Mason jar (right). Light olive. Screw cap. H. 5½ in. Rebner

Newspapers of the period carry irate letters and articles calling for the need for more sanitary conditions in dairy barns. Blame was placed on many different situations and one letter to an editor, written in 1880, complained that "Disease is not poured into milk with water, but comes from feeding rotten and dirty foods, or from filthy surroundings." Milk inspection by the government at the beginning of this century consisted of testing milk for the amount of solids it contained once it was delivered to the cities. Dirty backwoods barns, where cows were kept in the worst imaginable conditions, still existed at the turn of the century. Milk was delivered to market in carelessly washed cans where it was doled out to the consumer who carried it home in his own pail or jar.

The farmer's resistance to the added expense of pasteurizing milk meant that this process came into use later than it should have. The milk bottle was first used in the 1880s and it was not until just before the turn of the century that milk bottles appeared in any quantity. A Doctor Thatcher of New York invented a milk bottle in 1884 that used a Lightning-type closure made of metal. These bottles have an embossment of a Quaker farmer milking a cow and the embossed legend, "Absolutely Pure Milk, The Milk Protector" on them. Dr. Thatcher was responsible for the invention of the paper cap which brought the milk bottle into common usage in 1889.

Milk bottles were first made in a round shape; square and round squat bottles date after 1900. A milk bottle with a bulbous neck that was supposed to show off the high cream content of unhomogenized milk to better advantage was made in 1930 and was not used long.

Most milk bottles have been made in clear glass but there have been a few exceptions. Amber bottles have been used from time to time since they are known to minimize spoilage. Green was another color that was used by at least one dairy, Alta Crest Farms in Spencer, Massachusetts.

Hundreds of embossed pictures, many of them amusing and all of them interesting, can be found on the

LEFT: *Atlas "E-Z Seal" Fruit jar. "Bail here" embossed on neck. Clear. H. 7 in.* Author

RIGHT: *Ball "Ideal" Fruit jar. H. 7 in.* Author

earlier milk bottles. After a cheap method of permanent enamel labeling was discovered in the mid-1930s, embossments began to disappear.

There are still hundreds of related items for the collector of milk bottles to gather as collateral material. Many dairies sent out advertising items over the years as one method of keeping their route customers faithful. Now that milk is bottled in large central plants, the personal contact between the farmer and his customer no longer exists. Advertising items such as mugs, calendars, spoons, and even the obsolete paper caps will become more and more collectible. What may be pure nostalgia for the past today will become the historical relics of the future.

Food preservation before the nineteenth century was a constant problem. An early recipe for preserving pears will demonstrate to what lengths housewives went to offer a variety of food in the winter:

> Having prepared a number of earthenware jars, and a quantity of dry moss, place a layer of moss and pears alternately, till the jar is filled, then insert a plug, and seal around with melted rosin. These jars are sunk in dry sand to the depth of a foot; a deep cellar is preferable for keeping them to any fruit room. (*MacKenzie's 5000 Receipts*)

The earliest methods for keeping food in the winter mostly involved drying, burial in sand or pickling. Dry packing by the method quoted above was common. The foods were uncleaned and unprepared. A great deal of the food that was prepared and stored for the winter became unpalatable before fresh food was again available.

Nicolas Appert of France was the first to experiment with canning food in glass in response to a plea from the French government which realized that an *army traveled*

TOP: *Drey "Ever Seal" fruit jar. "Improved, Pat'd. 1920." Clear glass. H. 7½ in.* Author

BOTTOM: *Embossed milk or cream bottle. H. 7 in.* Rebner

on its stomach. Napoleon's army was in need of adequate food during the long winter campaigns. Louis Pasteur's experiments with wine and beer preservation led to the discovery that heat could be used to kill microbes. The idea of packing food in glass and heating it after the jar was sealed revolutionized the eating habits of Europe and America. One could now safely preserve palatable fruit and vegetables and enjoy them the year round.

Pasteur's experiments had proved that an absolutely airtight closure was necessary if food was not to spoil, and for a long time the glass manufacturers could not find a foolproof closure. Cork was the only practical means of stopping bottles that until around 1850 were not standardized in size. Wax or resin seals were used over the cork to prevent air from entering the jars, but a better type of seal was needed.

Glass fruit jars were made and advertised by Dr. Dyott around 1830, but Dyott's jars used cork closures. The first fruit jar closure that led to the invention of many others was of tin, but it still required a wax seal. This lid,

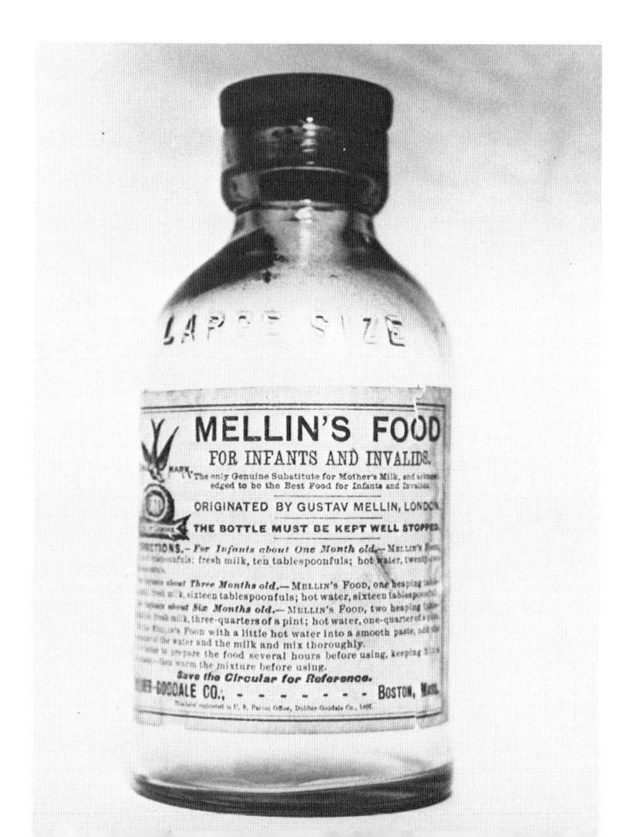

ABOVE: *Embossed milk or cream bottle. H. 7 in.* Rebner

LEFT: *Mellin's food for infants and invalids. Embossed "Large Size, Mellin's infant's food / Doliber-Goodale Co. / Boston." Aqua. H. 6½ in.* Rebner

RIGHT: *Nursing bottles and nipples were made in a great variety of shapes as this 1902 Sears Roebuck advertisement shows.*

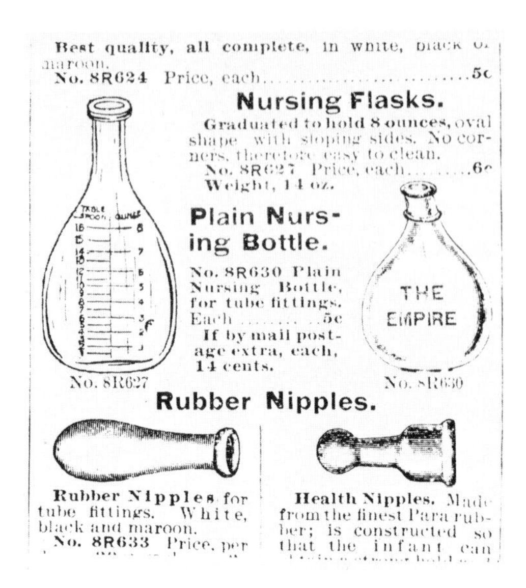

Best quality, all complete, in white, black or maroon.
No. 8R624 Price, each..............................5c

Nursing Flasks.

Graduated to hold 8 ounces, oval shape with sloping sides. No corners, therefore easy to clean.
No. 8R627 Price, each..........6c
Weight, 14 oz.

No. 8R627

Plain Nursing Bottle.

No. 8R630 Plain Nursing Bottle, for tube fittings. Each..........5c
If by mail postage extra, each, 14 cents.

THE EMPIRE

No. 8R630

Rubber Nipples.

Rubber Nipples for tube fittings. White, black and maroon.
No. 8R633 Price, per

Health Nipples. Made from the finest Para rubber; is constructed so that the infant can

BELOW: *Teal blue glass peppersauce bottle. H. 7⅞ in.*
Rebner

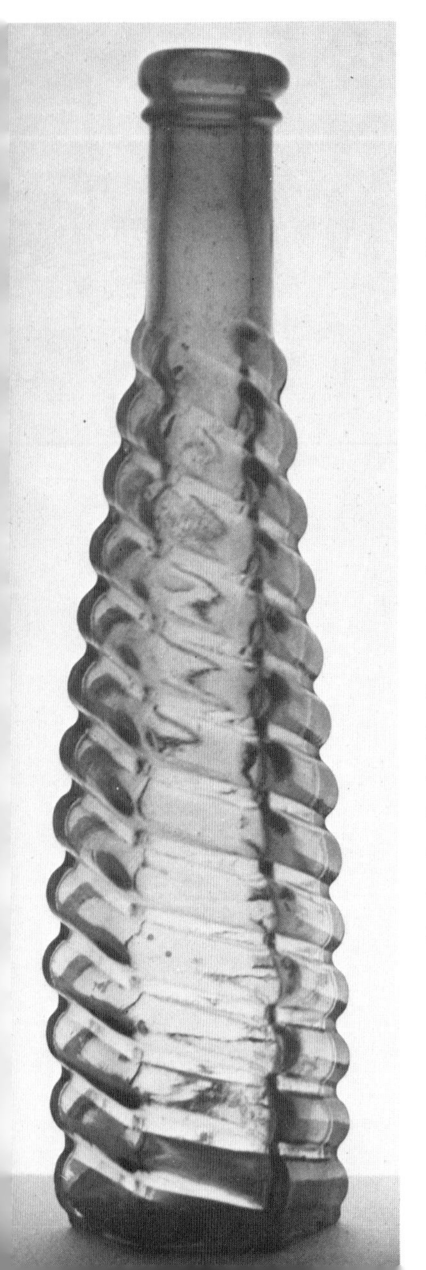

invented by Robert Arthur in 1855, fitted into a slot molded into the mouth of the jar.

The next important development in fruit jar closures came in 1858 when John Landis Mason, a tinsmith, patented a low cost screw-top fruit jar container and lid. Mason's lid was made of zinc and while the use of a screw thread molded into glass bottle lips was not new, Mason's jar was made with a wide mouth which made packing easier and his lid was airtight. One drawback was the use of zinc which was not a desirable material to use in close contact with food over a long period of time.

Attempts to improve on Mason's lid were made by others, notably a glass lid that was held on by a zinc screw-top patented by Salmon B. Rowley and Lewis Boyd, who inserted an opal glass liner in the Mason lid so that no metal came in contact with the food. Many other types of jars and closures were invented subsequently, but the name "Mason" became the generic term for glass jars used in home canning.

The magic of having rows of fruit and vegetables in

gleaming glass jars on hand to liven formerly dull winter menus led to the wide use of fruit jars in America. Commercially packed foods were generally unavailable until the beginning of this century. The reassuring rows of colorful food on shelves of the special cellar closets built into late nineteenth-century houses were a comfort to housewives who had slaved over hot stoves in the summer to lay in their winter preserves.

The collecting of fruit jars, which is relatively recent, is a category that appeals especially to women, since some remember the preserve closets and others remember with less nostalgia that fruit ripens in the hottest days of August and that the task of preserving it is difficult.

Even with the convenience of commercially canned food, home canning is still done in many parts of the country. Fruit jars that have been handed down from one generation to the next are still in use and it is probable that many interesting jars that have not yet been seen will come to light eventually.

Collectible fruit jars are those with interesting embossments such as "Gem," "The Queen," "King," "The Kalamazoo," "Lustre," "Presto," "Lightning," "Globe," "Fruitkeeper," and of course, "Mason" and "Ball." The old pottery jars can also be collected. Although glass fruit jars are for the most part made in clear or aqua glass, they can sometimes be found in colored glass. Black glass, milk glass, amber, emerald green and cobalt blue jars are truly collectible, and all but the amber are quite rare. Colored jars command very high prices and will obviously increase in value as this new category of bottle collecting becomes more popular.

The fruit jar collector can also gather together as collateral material early cookbooks and commercial booklets given away by the glassmakers as advertising. Various gadgets made to lighten the burden of the housewife as

Bottle embossed "The Great Atlantic and Pacific Tea Company, New York" was used for extracts. Sun-colored amethyst H. 5¾ in. Rebner

A bonanza for any bottle collector would be this box of unopened and labeled sweet oil bottles. Bottle height 10 in. c. 1880. Mattatuck

she cleaned, cooked, and packed pecks of produce are also sought.

There are, of course, many other food bottles and jars used around the home that can be collected. Olive oil and sweet oil bottles can be found, as well as those bottles that contained some of the earliest commercial food products such as mustard, pickles, catsup, and peppersauce. Bottles that have embossments of long established food chains or packers are of historical interest. Now that plastic has replaced a great many of the food bottles and jars with which we are familiar, it is probable that this sort of collecting will become more popular.

Many of the food bottles that can be found do not have any embossment, so that they may be difficult to identify. Because of this, any early food bottles found with labels are important for future identification.

Another type of bottle that contained food and was used domestically is the nursing bottle. Collectors have long been interested in feeding devices for babies and a wide variety of them exists. Since a practical rubber nipple was not devised until 1900, hundreds of types of bottles were made before this century with ingenious methods for getting food from the bottle to the baby's mouth. The bottles most likely to be found today, however, are the embossed ones produced in this century in a variety of shapes, many of which will not stand upright but are made to lie on their sides. Baby feeding bottles also have a great variety of interesting shapes and embossments which could interest collectors. Since glass has been almost totally replaced for baby bottles by the more practical unbreakable plastic, it will not be long before any glass baby bottles will be desirable.

Collateral material in this specialty are other feeding devices such as pap feeders, baby spoons, plates, mugs, and early magazine and newspaper articles on the care and feeding of babies.

ABOVE: *Garnier bottle, ceramic. Made in Italy. Replica of Eiffel Tower with other landmarks of Paris surrounding base. H. 13 in.*

ABOVE RIGHT: *Giunti and Figli majolica bottle for wine. Hand-painted. Made in Italy. H. 6½ in.*

RIGHT: *Garnier "Fiat 500–1934." 1959 crème de menthe bottle. Yellow and black ceramic. ⅔ pint. L. 8½ in.*

Chapter 22

NEW FIGURAL BOTTLES AND GIFT DECANTERS

ALTHOUGH no other gift decanters in novelty shapes have the popularity with collectors that Jim Beam bottles seem to have, there are many other distilleries that put their products in collectible figural bottles, some of which are of good quality and design. These contemporary bottles are constantly being watched for and evaluated by members of bottle clubs and become popular according to their scarcity and general appeal.

Most of the figural bottles that are used as gift decanters for alcoholic beverages are ceramic rather than glass. Some are issued in series for the collector and some are simply made to sell a particular product at a particular time. Other bottles are made in shapes that are a trademark of the firm.

Figural bottles are usually found in abundance at the larger liquor stores at Christmas time, making it necessary for the liquor dealer to be as much a connoisseur of pottery as he is of fine wines. The dealer who formerly had only to worry about strict government controls in dispensing alcoholic beverages in bottles now has the added

RIGHT: *Barsottini ceramic bottle. "Arc de Triomphe." Venicola, Florence, Italy. Holds red wine. H. 7¼ in. 1968.*

BELOW: *Ballantine's whiskey "Epic" series bottle. Series issued to celebrate 160th anniversary of distillers. White glass with ceramic finish. Gladiators are embossed on plastic insert in bottle depression on face. Background in insert is blue. Eagle on reverse. H. 9¼ in.*

BELOW RIGHT: *Ballantine's whiskey bottle: "Fisherman." Cream-colored with bright glaze. Made of "Genuine Palfrey China." H. 14 in.*

LEFT: *Coalport made this blue and white Delft type decanter for Harvey's Bristol Cream Sherry. H. 11¾ in.*

BELOW: *House of Koshu. Japanese sake bottle in figure of geisha. H. 12¼ in.*

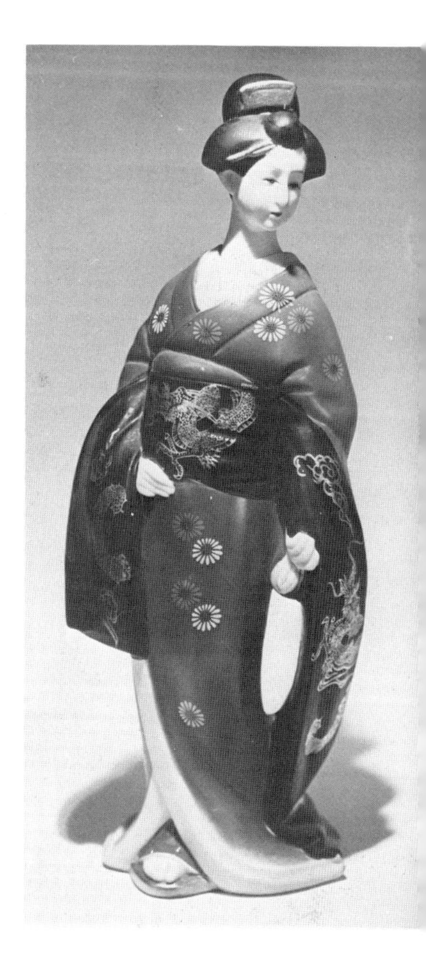

concern of whether he is going to be able to provide a favorite customer with a particular new figural bottle in time for the holidays.

Not all contemporary collectible bottles are for liquor. The popularity of the bottle collecting hobby has induced manufacturers to produce empties just for the collector. These bottles have the advantage in that they can be advertised in bottle magazines and newspapers and sold through the mail. The words, "Limited Edition," are enough to sell new novelty bottles in large quantities. It is seldom the buyer is informed just how "limited" the "edition" is, nor does he seem to care. In cases where only a few bottles really are issued, prices soar soon after the bottle is announced.

For the older figural bottles that were made before there were so many bottle collectors, prices are the highest. The law of "supply and demand" holds for these bottles as well as for other early ones. Because there are so many avid collectors, the demand for any interesting, novel or pretty bottle is high, especially if it is also scarce.

A great many collectible bottles of the figural type were made before the Beam bottles came on the scene. Many of the ceramic bottles were made by well-known potters in Europe to order for liquor firms and distilleries. Some of these older bottles are very rare and sought after not only by bottle collectors, but also by ceramics enthusiasts who specialize in a particular kind of pottery. A commercial bottle made by Wedgwood, for instance, in the 1920s, has two groups of collectors competing for the few remaining specimens, each of whom wants it for different reasons.

Both beautiful and ugly bottles can be found in the category of figural and gift bottles. Collectors are on the whole less concerned with aesthetics than they are with rarity. To collectors, the scarcest bottles are the best, and it is the one that is most difficult to find that is the most in demand and brings the highest prices.

Liqueurs, whiskey, wines, and cordials are the products most likely to be packaged in interesting and expensive ceramic bottles. The Luxardo Company of Torreglia,

ABOVE: *Dant Distillery "Boston Tea Party" white glass. Dant "Americana" series. H. 9 in.*

LEFT: *"Mountie" Canadian Mist bottle made by Barton Porcelain Company in a limited edition. "Fine Figurine" series. H. 14 in. 1969.*

RIGHT: *Kentucky Gentleman "Soldier" series. Ceramic. H. 14 in. 1969.*

LEFT: *Old Cabin Still Kentucky Straight Bourbon Whiskey. "Genuine porcelain" impressed on bottom. "Collector's Gallery" series. H. 11¼ in. 1963.*

RIGHT: *Metaxa, Greek liqueur, was bottled in this china figural. Shirt has glass buttons. H. 18 in. 1970.*

Italy, has bottled its wines and liqueurs in ceramic bottles of good quality and design for thirty-five years. Many of these bottles have been exported to this country. Luxardo also has used a Venetian glass firm to make gift decanters for their products and some of these do have redeeming artistic characteristics. In contrast to most American-made figural and gift bottles, the Luxardo bottles are often handmade or hand-decorated.

A French firm, the P. Garnier Company, has been bottling some of its products in figural bottles since the late 1930s and some of these are in great demand by collectors. The ceramics are novel and amusing and many of them are hand-decorated.

Ballantine Scotch was bottled in milk glass containers in a series called "Epic" issued to commemorate the 160th anniversary of Distiller George Ballantine. There are four bottles in this series and they are currently being collected. Ballantine also issued a "Limited Edition" bottle of a fisherman made of Palfrey China that has the distinction of not being able to stand on a shelf. The

RIGHT: *Ezra Brooks bottle, ceramic, 1968. "Made of Genuine Heritage China." H. 7¾ in. L. 6¾ in.*

BELOW: *Ezra Brooks engine. Black, gold, and red glazed china. H. 8 in. L. 9¾ in.*

LEFT: *"Liberty Bell" issued by Ezra Brooks. Heritage China. H. 8¼ in. 1969.*

RIGHT: *Black and white Scotch Whiskey. Black Scottie dog issued along with another of white china. Made of Royal Adderley English Bone China. Holds fifth of Scotch. 1970.*

fisherman is made in a sitting position and can only be placed on the edge of a shelf or table.

The J. W. Dant Distillery of Kentucky has made a great many ceramic and glass bottles of the figural, novelty or commemorative type in recent years. Other bourbon distillers have followed suit. Competition among American distilleries seems to be for the bottle trade rather than the drinking crowd.

At no time in bottle history have there been issued so many figural, historical or commemorative bottles. All bottlers, eager to cater to the collectors' enthusiasm for bottles that are new and different, have taxed their designers' imaginations to the point of absurdity. Whiskey in fancy decanters is advertised as though the bottles were a bonus or a gift of the distillery. This is far from the truth. Often the buyer must pay many times the value of the alcoholic drink advertised in order to own the "limited edition" china scottie dog or the replica of the colonial soldier. However, if the numbers made of that one particular bottle are truly limited, the collector knows that his investment is probably safe.

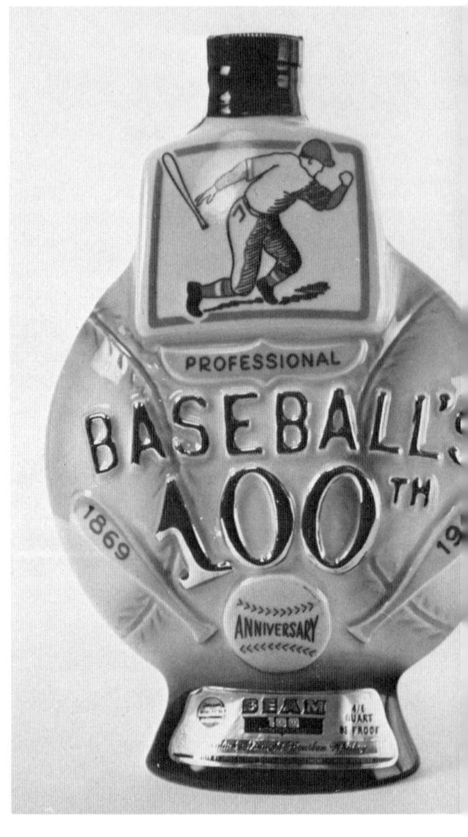

ABOVE: *Beam's "South Carolina Tricentennial" bottle. Regal China. H. 9 in.*

ABOVE RIGHT: *Beam's "Baseball's 100th Anniversary" bottle. Regal China. H. 10¼ in.*

RIGHT: *Beam's "Pimlico Race Course, Preakness" bottle. Regal China. 11½ in. 1970.*

Chapter 23

JIM BEAM BOTTLES

IT should be obvious by now to all bottle enthusiasts that fancy commercial bottles are used where the liquid they contain is so much like competitors' products that the package itself must be the attraction for the buyer. Fancy gift containers for alcoholic beverages are a twentieth-century phenomenon. The buyer, reaching for a fifth of bourbon or rye will often pick the prettiest bottle on the shelf when he is buying it for a gift. When the bottle begins to sell the product, the distiller knows he has a winner. He also has two profits instead of one. The customer pays for the gift decanter in most cases.

The James B. Beam Distilling Company of Kentucky, an old bourbon distillery (now owned by the American Tobacco Company), issued their first gift bottle, a glass cocktail shaker, in 1953. The popularity of this first gift bottle, issued for the Christmas season, led to the manufacture of commemorative bottles in series that are released one at a time. In the Jim Beam series are "Trophies," "Politicals," "Executives," "States," "Centennials," "Customer Specialties," "Regal China Specialties," and "Glass

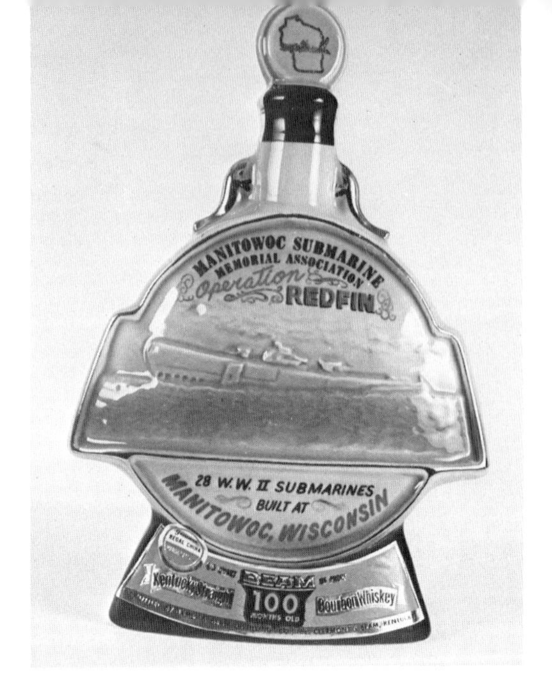

LEFT: *"Germany" from Beam's "Country" series. Map of Germany on reverse side. H. 10¼ in.*

RIGHT: *Bottle commemorating Manitowoc Submarine Memorial Association issued by Beam. Regal China. H. 11½ in. 1970.*

Specialties." Within these, and other, categories are bottles that are made to be collected.

Since the historic cocktail shaker of 1953 the Jim Beam Distillery has issued over two hundred novelty bottles and more are being added all the time. Beam Bottle Clubs have mushroomed across the country, books and pamphlets have quickly gone to press listing the bottles issued by the company, and prices on those most difficult to find, and therefore, the most desirable, have risen to staggering heights.

There are few historical flasks that demand the high price, for instance, of the Regal China Beam bottle, "The First National Bank of Chicago," which was issued in 1964. This bottle was made to order in a limited amount and is a rarity. At this point it might be as well to point out that a "rarity" in the category of the Beam bottles does not mean that there are only several or even ten in existence. It simply means that there are a lot less of a particular bottle than there are of others. Since there are so many Beam collectors whose aim it is to gather every bottle the company has issued since 1953, there are not enough of each bottle to satisfy all collectors. The "Customer Specialties" series, made to order in limited amounts that were not in general distribution, are the Beam bottles that usually bring the highest prices.

One desirable category of Jim Beam bottles are those ceramic bottles made by the Regal China Company of Illinois. This company's sole product is the variety of bottles made for the Beam Distillery. There are many figural bottles included in the Regal China list. In the "Trophy" series are ducks, fish, pheasants, horses, foxes, does, eagles, cats, bluejays, robins, and woodpeckers. Bottles shaped like the states they commemorate, replicas of buildings or coins, a china slot machine, cartoon characters of the Republican elephant and the Democratic donkey are some of the popular figurals on the Beam list. Overly baroque decanters with heavy gilding and embossing that are fancifully named "Marbled Fantasy," "Royal Rose," "Blue Cherub," "Majestic," and "Prestige" are also favorite Beams conjured up by Regal.

Regional historic events, many of a minor nature that might never have been heard of nationally, are commemorated on Beam bottles to be found on liquor store shelves across the country. A "Collector's Edition" with prints of American paintings adorning fuzzy flocked glass bottles have been turned out in several series.

Viewed from an artistic point of view, there is little to recommend most Jim Beam bottles as worth collecting. Many of the Regal bottles are garish and viewed from the ceramicist's point of view, singularly badly designed. Yet the number of Beam collectors has grown to such proportions in the past few years that prices for many of the bottles have multiplied over and over.

The answer to the Beam enigma is that the bottles are made to cater to the collector's urge to own things in

Beam Elks bottle from Centennial series. Regal China. H. 11 in. Issued 1968–69.

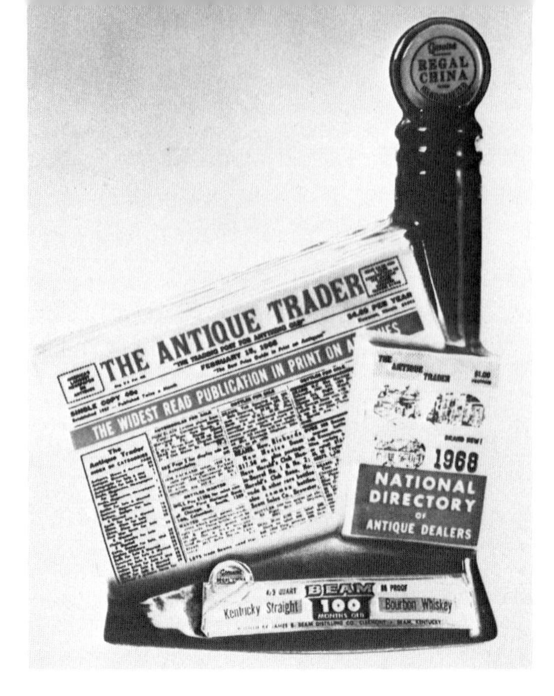

Beam bottle for The Antique Trader, *a newspaper that specializes in bottle advertising for collectors. Regal China. H. 10½ in. 1968.*

limited series. The information about this area of bottle collecting is complete and is constantly kept up to date through the many collectors' newspapers and bottle club newsletters that have been founded throughout the country in the past few years. The Beam Distillery would be foolish if they did not know a good thing when they had it, and they promote their bottles more aggressively than they do their product. The bottles are novelties that are being purchased and extolled by dealers and collectors as though they were works of art.

What the Beam Distillery has provided is an easily identifiable collector's item, in somewhat limited quantity, with a wide variety of shapes and colors. They make a great many regional bottles that appeal to citizens of those regions. The psychology of the collector personality is catered to by the issuing of dated bottles in series. The urge to complete series collections and the hunt for the bottles that are difficult to find, or expensive, well strong in the collector's personality. Of course, it is probable that most of the Beam bottle collectors see redeeming artistic values in these bottles. However, in any collecting fad there is always the danger that the objects that rise in value so swiftly are being promoted falsely by dealers who see a profitable market ahead. For the collector who needs new stoppers for Beam bottles or new labels, these are available through advertisements in collectors' newspapers. Privately printed booklets listing all Beam bottles along with current market prices are also available.

That the bottle collecting craze that is currently sweeping America should manifest itself in this totally manufactured and contrived category of collecting is an interesting phenomenon that will only be placed in its proper perspective with the passage of time. One cannot help but wonder whether future generations of Americans will give the Regal China Company's "First National Bank of Chicago" the respect that current enthusiasts seem to heap upon it. Those who have invested large amounts of time and money in these novelty bottles should bear in mind the media limitations in advertising imposed in America on whiskey manufacturers and consider whether the novelty bottles have been the most desirable means of pushing a product that a distillery could ever hope for.

LEFT: *Beam decanter made by Regal China Co. Gray, yellow, blue, and gold. H. 12¼ in.*

RIGHT: *Beam's Glass specialties with print of "Whistler's Mother" on blue flocked glass. H. 10¼ in.*

TOP LEFT: *Avon bottle for cologne. "The Capitol." Amber with gold dome. H. 5½ in. 1970.* Palmieri

RIGHT: *Avon bottle in shape of hitching-post. Green glass with gold cap and ring. H. 5¾ in.* Palmieri

BOTTOM LEFT: *Avon perfume bottle. "Petit Fleur." Clear glass, gold cap. H. 3 in. 1968.* Palmieri

RIGHT: *Avon "Bell" is made of clear ribbed glass with gold metallic handle. Center of bottle is hollow and clapper is real bell. Made for cologne. H. 5 in. 1968.* Palmieri

Chapter 24

AVON BOTTLES

ONE type of American-made bottle for perfume and other cosmetics that is highly suitable for collecting is the Avon bottle. Avon Products, Inc. of New York originated in 1883 under the name of the California Perfume Company. From its beginning the company has sold its products through a network of saleswomen (and some men) door-to-door. The name of the company was changed to Allied Products in 1930 and to Avon, after a popular fragrance the company had made, in 1939. Avon Products are sold throughout the United States and in many other countries as well.

It would seem that with the wide distribution Avon products have enjoyed for many years that there would be no shortage of the bottles in which their cosmetics have been packaged and therefore, no reason for collectors to become so enthusiastic about collecting them. However, Avon bottles have been made in thousands of styles and anyone limiting himself to the collection of bottles of just this one company usually finds himself

Avon bottle for after-shave lotion: "Bowling Pin." White glass with red bands. H. 6½ in. Palmieri

further curtailing his collection by choosing just one or two categories of Avons.

Since Avon bottle collecting is fairly recent, many of the bottles that are collected are also not old. Because some of the newer bottles are more desirable than others the prices vary considerably for some very recent Avons. Most of the bottles are elaborate in design and the majority of them are figural representations of the name of the cosmetic they hold.

Avon bottles are made in the New England area by various companies, but are designed by Avon factory designers. It was not the Avon Company's original plan that their bottles would become collectors' items, although they now issue bottles that are labeled "Collector's Item" and products are packaged in designs that are issued in series so that the customer can collect groups of similar bottles.

The cult of Avon collectors has spread to the point where almost every Avon customer and saleslady saves the bottles. The Avon Company has been astute in recognizing a good thing and it continues to issue bottles that will appeal to their customers.

Avon representatives, who must count on their own circles of friends and relatives for repeat business, are given a limited line of products that are constantly packaged in new bottles and called by another name. Repeated changes in packaging are extremely important for continuing sales. New products, or old ones that are called by a new name and come in a different bottle, are offered every two weeks. At the same time the Avon Ladies are sent a "special," which is a product in a container that has been off the market and is reintroduced in a limited quantity for a limited time. Sometimes the "special" is a new product in a newly designed container made in limited quantities. Collectors watch for these "specials," hoping to corner the market on a desirable bottle that might become scarce within a very short time.

Because of Avon's policy of constantly changing package design, there are hundreds of figural bottles, many in series or types that are similar enough to form a collection when completed. Antique automobiles, book decanters, and other figurals are collected in groups.

The collecting craze that has grown around Avon figural bottles has created an interesting situation for the Avon executives who are responsible for it. A recent CAMPAIGN REMINDER, a newsletter sent to district representatives of the company, stated "Our business is cosmetics and toiletries, not bottles." Evidently the Avon Company has been besieged with requests for information on the history of their bottles. They also state in the same letter that they cannot identify and authenticate old bottles. They say that "Avon was founded back in 1886, and it would be practically impossible to put together a complete list and description of the thousands of different bottles we've made since then . . . or to sup-

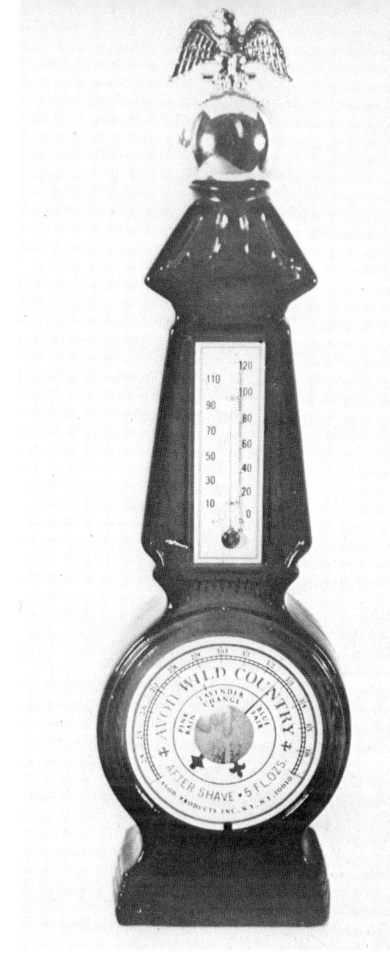

ABOVE: *Barometer bottle by Avon is called "Weather or Not" and is made in amber glass. Holds after-shave lotion. H. 9½ in. 1969.* Palmieri

LEFT: *Avon has made a series of eight automobiles of antique vintage. This one is "Straight Eight" and is made of green glass. Closure is plastic trunk. For after-shave lotion. L. 6½ in.* Palmieri

TOP: *Avon "Sterling Six," made of amber glass. Spare tires are plastic and screw off. Avon autos have recently been reissued. L. 6 in. 1968.* Palmieri

BOTTOM: *Avon "Electric Charger" after-shave bottle. Black glass with red plastic trunk closure. L. 6 in.* Palmieri

ply old bottles requested by collectors." Avon does admit, however, that they are flattered that people across the country have found Avon bottles and decanters so attractive that they are collecting them as a hobby. It is interesting that recent television advertising of Avon products stresses the bottles somewhat more than the product.

Many of the products made by the company before it was called "Avon" are now in demand by collectors. When these bottles are found unopened and in their original boxes, they are the most prized of all Avon bottles. One of the reasons that Avons appeal to a large amount of collectors is that they represent a company that has become enormously successful and profitable by peddling its product in an original manner and packaging it in unique ways.

The Avon bottle designers' imaginations are taxed to the limit when new bottles must be designed with such frequency, and those responsible for naming the package and the product must come up with new ideas constantly. Avon bottles are known to collectors by such easily identifiable names as "Miss Lollypop," "Majorette Boot," "Golden Apple Perfumed Candle Container" (a frosted metallic glass apple which held perfume), "Daylight Shaving Time" (a gold metal bottle shaped like a pocket watch which held after-shave cologne), and "Dollars and Scents" (a white glass bottle shaped like a roll of bills with a green raised design). A bottle called "Decisions, Decisions" held after-shave lotion and had a cap at either end. "20 Paces" is a set of two bottles shaped as, you guessed it, duelling pistols!

Avon bottles in the shapes of a gavel, a snail, a set of golf clubs, a football helmet, a scimitar, a stein, a town

LEFT: *Avon "Solid Gold Cadillac" after-shave bottle. L. 7¼ in.* Curulla

RIGHT: *Avon bottle in shape of bird made for perfume. Frosted glass with gold cap. L. 1¼ in.* Palmieri

pump, a barometer or a bell are all favored by collectors. Christmas tree ornament bottles are issued at the appropriate time of year and a series of cartoon character bottles that once held children's cosmetics are in demand as collectible objects too.

The Avon representative, who heretofore only had to worry about the discontinuance of a product such as "Cosmic Blue and White Cake Eyeliner" now must concern herself with supplying collectors with enough "Easter Bonnet Bunny" bottles. Because Avon bottles are worth more to collectors when they are unopened, it is probable that a lot of Avon toiletries do not get used any more.

The Avon Company, which at one time issued bottles more than once and still reissue a bottle design occasionally, will have to worry about whether it is worth antagonizing collectors by making a bottle that had become rare a second time without marking it in some way. While Avon has reissued bottles and decanters that have sold particularly well in the past, the company cannot

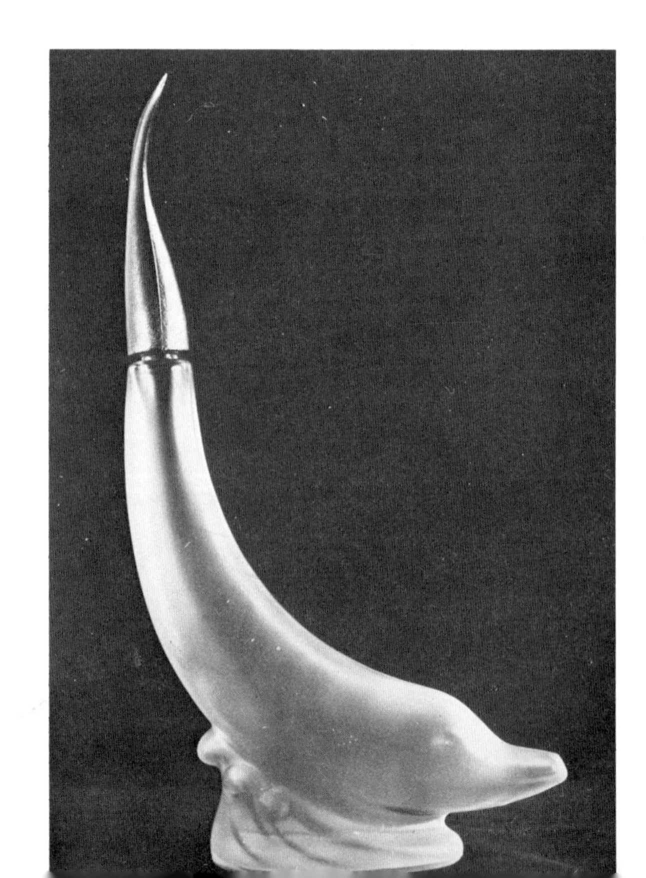

ABOVE: *Avon "Sea Horse" in clear glass with Florentine finish gold cap. H. 7¼ in.* Curulla

RIGHT: *Frosted glass dolphin with gold metallic cap made for "Skin-so-Soft" bath oil. H. 10½ in.* Curulla

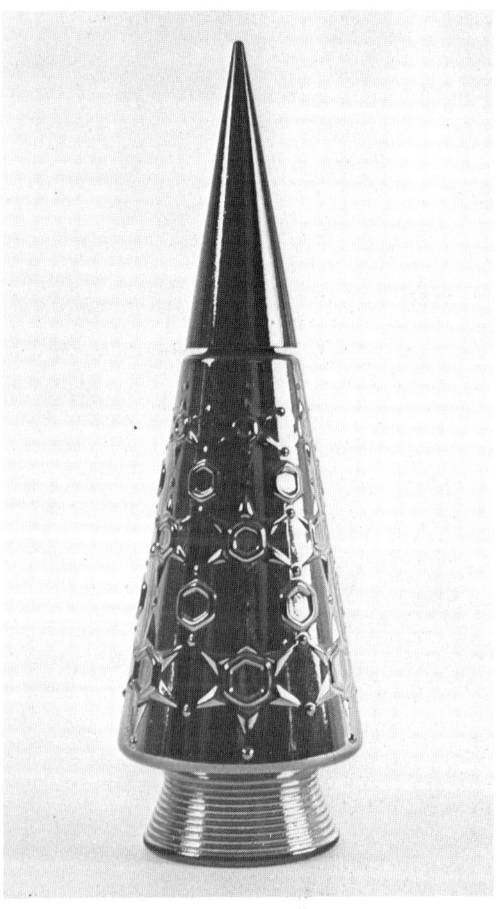

help but concern itself with a great percentage of their loyal customers who now buy the bottle rather than the product. When the Avon lady calls, she is now selling collectible bottles as well as soap, perfume, and dusting powder. She also is the source of related items which avid Avon collectors love. Her catalogs, sales pamphlets, delivery bags, and other paraphernalia are collateral material that is in constant demand by collectors.

LEFT: *Realistic old-fashioned telephone was made to hold two products, talc in the receiver and after-shave lotion in the bottle itself. Gold finished glass with black plastic receiver. H. 8½ in.* Palmieri

RIGHT: *Avon "Christmas Tree" bubble bath. Tree-shaped bottle came in metallic red, green, gold, and silver. H. 7 in. 1968.* Curulla

TOP: *New reproduction of "Booz" bottle is made for collectors and sold as decorative bottle. The new version is produced automatically. Mark embossed on bottom of reproduction bottle (shown at left) is imitation pontil mark.* Calabrese

RIGHT: *Two reproduction bitters bottles made in variety of colors. These bottles are produced to be used decoratively, but will become collectors' items of the future.* Calabrese

Chapter 25

REPRODUCTIONS AND NEW HISTORICAL FLASKS

UNTIL recently, when collectors' desire for old bottles became so strong, there had been little point in reproducing many of the old bottles that are now in demand. The earlier collectors of old bottles had little to worry about as far as fakes and reproductions were concerned. While some bottles have been reproduced in the past, most were honest reproductions and not an attempt to fool the buyer. Some of these reproductions are as valuable to the collector today as the original bottle was. Any successful design can be reproduced if it is sold as a reproduction and if no attempt is made by the seller to pass the item off as anything but new.

Considering the many categories of bottle collecting, there are not many types of old bottles that have, until recently, been worth copying in order to sell new bottles as originals. Some of the early historical flasks have, of course, been reproduced from time to time, but usually these have been honest reproductions. The E. C. Booz log-cabin bottle has been reproduced several times in the last hundred years and is currently being made again.

However, anyone who is aware of the qualities of old glass and the methods used to make blown bottles could not confuse the new bottle with the old.

The embossed bottles of the latter half of the nineteenth century have not, until recently, had enough value for anyone to reproduce them. Therefore, bottles of this type are a very safe investment for today's collector. The few bitters and medicine bottles that are being reproduced are not blown and therefore, are easy to detect as new.

In the category of early wine bottles and unmarked carboys and demijohns, these utilitarian bottles are still being made in various parts of the world, notably Italy and Mexico. Importers have been selling these recently as reproductions, but they are difficult for the novice collector to identify as new. It is possible that this type of bottle will soon find its way to flea markets or auctions where they will be sold as old bottles.

Because bottle collectors are interested in any unusual bottles, whether new or old, a few series of historical bottles have been introduced recently that are fast becoming collectors' items. These bottles are made with the interests of the collector in mind and are sold empty. They are made in limited editions and prices of the discontinued designs have been soaring. Perhaps the most noteworthy of these is the Wheaton-Nuline series of presidential decanters. These bottles, with likenesses of some of our more recent presidents, continue the tradition of making flasks with portraits that began at the beginning of the nineteenth century. The most popular bottle in this series is a blue John F. Kennedy bottle with the late President in profile. Other Presidents in this series are Franklin D. Roosevelt (green), Dwight D. Eisenhower (amethyst), Abraham Lincoln (topaz), Woodrow Wilson (dark blue), George Washington (frosted

"American Army Bitters," "Horseshoe Bitters," and "Jamaica Ginger Root Bitters" bottles are all faithful reproductions of early bitters bottles which, if genuine, would be quite valuable.
Calabrese

white), and Theodore Roosevelt (cobalt blue).

Another series of decanters made especially for collectors is called, "Great Americans." Martin Luther King, Robert Kennedy, Douglas MacArthur, Charles Lindbergh, Thomas Edison, Robert E. Lee, Will Rogers, Betsy Ross, Ben Franklin, and Billy Graham are commemorated in this series. There are also astronaut bottles. Then there are two political campaign bottles representing the two major parties; these are figural bottles with the elephant sporting portraits of Richard Nixon and Spiro Agnew, and with the donkey carrying the portraits of Hubert Humphrey and Edmund Muskie. It is likely that these new portrait flasks will eventually become important additions to collections of old portrait flasks.

Other types of bottles that have been recently reproduced are some of the early bitters bottles, food jars and ink bottles. Copies of the early milk bottles with porcelain caps, which were not used on milk bottles, are being made in Italy as well as miniatures of nineteenth-century patent medicine bottles with "authentic" labels. Most of these bottles are clearly marked with the manufacturer's name or the place of manufacture when they have been made abroad. However, it is not difficult to remove undesirable embossments and the collector should be aware of the alterations that can make a new bottle or its label look old. While currently these bottles are being sold as honest reproductions, there is little doubt that some novice collectors will be offered these bottles as old in the near future.

As bottle collecting becomes more and more popular as a hobby and the old desirable bottles become more difficult to find, there is little doubt that many reproductions will be sold as old bottles. The most ideal way to find old bottles is to dig them oneself. Barring that, purchase only from dealers you feel you can trust. It behooves any dealers in old and antique items to be knowledgeable about the things he sells and most established dealers will guarantee their sales as to age, value, and, in some cases, provenance.

Chapter 26

RELATIVE VALUES OF COLLECTIBLE BOTTLES

PRICE lists for the various categories of bottle collecting can be misleading. The market for bottles, old or nearly new, fluctuates considerably simply because collecting is a comparatively new hobby and many bottles that were, at first, considered difficult to find have a way of turning up in surprising numbers once they have been designated as rare and, therefore, high-priced. Once enough of these "rare" bottles are placed on the market, the price, of course, goes down.

An interesting fact about bottle literature is that within the past five or six years at least a hundred pamphlets and books have been written, mostly by collectors, listing specialized kinds of bottles and including price guides. Now that bottle collecting has become so widespread, there becomes a problem of what is available in what quantity in what region of the country. Many of the embossed bottles, for instance, are very regional. A soda bottle that may be found in quantity in Connecticut would be considered rare in California. Although embossed California whiskey bottles are in great demand in

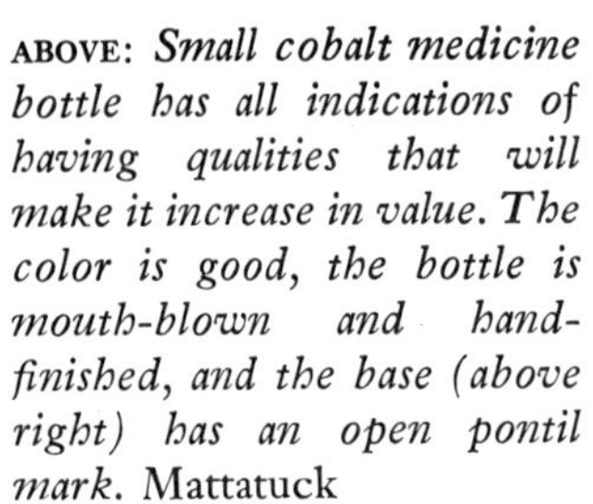

ABOVE: *Small cobalt medicine bottle has all indications of having qualities that will make it increase in value. The color is good, the bottle is mouth-blown and hand-finished, and the base (above right) has an open pontil mark.* Mattatuck

RIGHT: *This small Stiegel-type pocket flask in amethyst is a blown bottle that will constantly increase in value. H. 4⅞ in.* Mattatuck

Finds for any collector would be these Steigel-type perfume bottles in cobalt complete with original stoppers. Both are pontilled. Left bottle: h. 5¼ in. Right bottle: h. 5¾ in.
Mattatuck

the West, New Englanders have, as yet, little interest in these bottles. There are a great many older bottles that are of more interest to Eastern collectors.

New England bottle collectors have yet to become as fond of Avon or Jim Beam bottles to the degree that Western collectors have and many find the price guides for these bottles ludicrous. Since prices do not really stabilize for any collectible items until enough have been bought and sold and, most important, auctioned, it would be presumptuous on the part of any writer to conclude that the price of these new bottles had become stable.

In the matter of early bottles such as Stiegel or Pitkin-type pocket flasks or the historical flasks, there has been enough interest over a long enough period of time for dealers and buyers to be aware of which ones are rare and difficult to find. Also, enough of these bottles have been auctioned so that an average price can be taken. Because glass collectors and scholars have studied these older bottles over a period of fifty years, it is not difficult

Of these three "gift" decanters, only the bottle on the far right will increase in value to any great extent. Marked "Baccarat, France," it held Courvoisier brandy and is heavy, superior glass. Author

to believe that certain bottles will bring justifiably high prices.

The old American flasks and bottles have all the qualities of collectible items that lead one to believe that they will never lose their popularity among the knowledgeable. The flasks and bottles made by the eighteenth- and early nineteenth-century American glass houses have antique value, they are currently difficult to find, they required a great deal of skill and handwork in their manufacture, and—in the case of the historical and pictorial flasks—they are decorated with motifs of historical importance.

In the case of the early bitters bottles, the same is also mostly true. They too have been collected for a long time, many have artistic as well as historical value and prices for these bottles have become fairly stable. This does not mean that prices for both these categories do not rise, but they rise gradually and usually maintain the same relative values.

Later embossed bottles have no less charm than many

of the earlier bottles. They, too, are of historic importance and, for the most part, have a kind of beauty that is granted any early glass. The problem that exists as far as assessing the monetary value of these bottles is that there are so many different kinds made over a long period of time and it will be a long while before it is known which are truly rare and, therefore, more desirable. Interest in these bottles is so recent that it is almost an affront for any writer to assume that his price list for these bottles should be accepted as valid.

Souvenir bottles gain in value as they get older. This flask from 1933 Chicago World's Fair will constantly gain in value. Rebner

Old and beautiful scent bottles or blown three-mold decanters, both scarce now and highly collectible, can no longer be found at bargain prices. These artistically designed and made objects will probably never decrease in value. This is true of most good decorative bottles. Apothecary jars, drug bottles, and barber bottles representative of the various types of decorative glass made at the turn of the century can also be included in the same category. Bottles that were comparatively expensive to begin with will always bring high prices once they are in demand and have been documented. When these bottles were made by companies noted for high quality such as Tiffany, Baccarat or Lalique, one should have no concern about the safety of his investment.

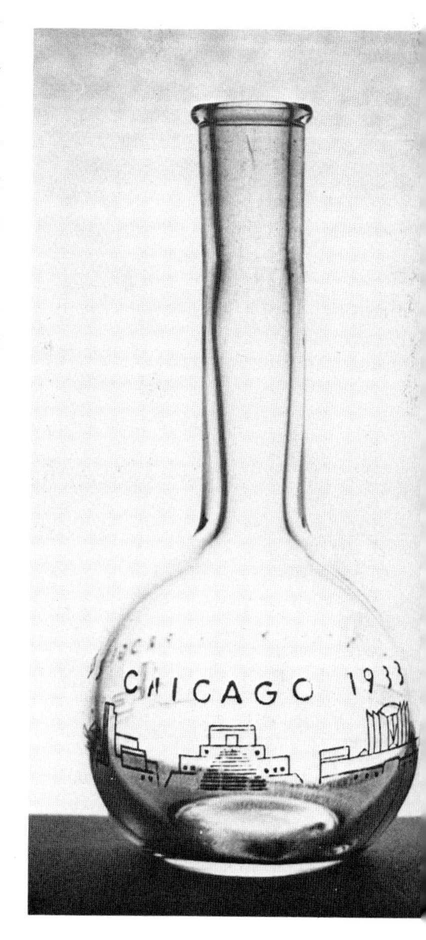

Commercial containers that have had a short life span, such as certain rare fruit jars or milk bottles, may increase enormously in value in the coming years but there is no way we can be certain. Although many are very desirable today and bring rather high prices, this is no proof that these same bottles are the ones that will be proven by history to be the more desirable collectors' items.

Various desirable embossments on many bottles raise prices but again it is difficult to know at this point how many of the same bottle exist. Prices for any collectible objects may be set by price guides only temporarily. Only

the passage of time will reveal how accurate these guides are. One should keep in mind that there are thousands of bottle collectors who are helping preserve many of the more important bottles of the nineteenth century. More and more bottles are being dug every day. While this is a very good thing and an enjoyable hobby for many it does keep up the supply of old bottles.

In the case of new collectible bottles, there is also a danger of there being an oversupply in future years for the prices to stay at their currently high level. It would be a good idea for any collector about to make a sizable investment in a new bottle of a "limited edition" to attempt to find out how many of that particular bottle have been made, since the information might have a great bearing on its future value.

Determining the price one should pay for any collectible item is simply a matter of how much one wants the object and what the market is for it. The rule, as always, must be "supply and demand." For attractive, collectible bottles the demand will always be there if present interest is any indication. In deciding which bottles will be wanted in the future, one should concern himself with the present "supply." When there are many of any object in existence, interest often begins to wane.

Figural bottles are all in demand by collectors. This candy container, one of many figurals made for that purpose in the first part of this century, is valuable to those who specialize in this field. Rebner

Chapter 27

HOW TO DISPLAY COLLECTIBLE BOTTLES

THERE are many types of bottles and probably almost as many sizes and types of collections. Any determined and acquisitive collector eventually faces the problem of how to display his collection to its best advantage. This is as true of the collector of decorative decanters as it is of the collector of fruit jars.

The first bottles to be collected and displayed in this country were the colorful and interesting historical and pictorial flasks. A common sight in New England for many years has been the farmhouse window with groups of colorful flasks lined up on the window sill. The informal architecture of the salt box house is a perfect background for old bottles that were made in the East.

A playroom or library can be enhanced when a collection of early bottles is displayed on shelves against a wall or on glass shelves built across a window. Historical flasks can be seen to their best advantage when displayed against a mirrored wall or window where the sunshine enhances their color.

The most ideal place for a large collection of bottles

RIGHT: *Powder or dresser jar of English cut glass with a silver cap is decorative today for many purposes. No longer relegated to the boudoir, it can be used on desks or end tables as decoration.* Hardy

BELOW: *This fancy apothecary bottle made by the Whitall Tatum Co. has found a new use as candy container. It is both decorative and practical. c. 1900.* Mattatuck

from the point of view of the housekeeper, is in an enclosed glass cabinet. Since most bottle collectors seem to amass as many examples of bottles as they can find, the problem of dust soon becomes pressing. If an entire household is not as fond of bottles as the collector, a lighted and enclosed glass front cabinet may help keep the peace. It will also diminish the chance of mishaps and lessen the necessity for frequent cleaning.

Many bottles can be used decoratively in different rooms in the home, such as old glass apothecary jars which will fit into almost any room in the home. Filled with brightly colored hard candy, these jars are decorative as well as useful. An apothecary jar is also an excellent place in which to display a collection of old glass marbles or shards that have been dug near glass houses.

An accomplished flower arranger can make attractive dried flower arrangements inside a clear drug jar. This type of flower arrangement is worth taking special pains over, since it will be dust-free in the wide-mouthed covered jar and will last indefinitely. One should use flowers and other dried material that are in scale with the size of the jar and insert the stems in a piece of styrofoam that has been anchored to the bottom of the jar with a little florist's clay. The styrofoam base can be covered with sphagnum moss once the arrangement is completed.

Pottery bottles and jugs have long been one of the flower arranger's favorite type of container. The texture of early stoneware is informal and most often of a neutral color so that any kind of flower may be used. Simple bouquets of field flowers look fresh and inviting in stoneware bottles or jugs.

Fruit jars and old milk bottles are finding their way back to the kitchen these days as useful as well as decorative objects. The glass-covered fruit jars, many of which are collectible but not yet of enormous value, are being displayed on the kitchen counter in place of canister sets. After a lifetime of plastic, America's young housewives have rediscovered the usefulness of fruit jars as a method of storing food. Easy to fill and wash, airtight and nostalgically attractive, the popularity of glass fruit jars as kitchen decoration will grow.

Bottles may be used decoratively in many ways. Widemouthed jars are used to hold colorful bars of soap in the bathroom; a shelf of old embossed medicine bottles can be displayed in the same room. The large black glass demijohns and carboys are decorative on a terrace or patio and are as interesting a focal point as a piece of sculpture. A collection of embossed whiskey bottles is attractive and at home on a shelf in a playroom or game room. Perfume bottles grouped together are an attractive bedroom accessory.

Collateral material such as trade cards, labels, and advertisements can become wall decorations if they are properly grouped together, matted and placed in nineteenth-century frames. In recent years the paper ephemera of the past has become a popular way of enlivening the surfaces of walls. Old advertising posters and bitters or medicine bottle labels have a special meaning for the bottle collector.

Chemist's bottle with hollow-knob stopper is decorative object when filled with a shell collection. Author

ABOVE: *Ancient Egyptian glass shows extreme case of sick glass. A beautiful opalescent color, the glass is flaking from the surface due to oxidation.* Mattatuck

RIGHT: *Dirt particles on inner surface of this old bottle can be removed by patient soaking and washing.* Rebner

Chapter 28

THE CLEANING, CARE, AND REPAIR OF OLD BOTTLES

A NEWLY dug bottle seldom resembles anything that anyone would want to display in his house. Years of grime and dirt cling to glass with a tenacity equalled only by the determination of the finder to restore his precious bottle to pristine condition. Before the initial cleaning it is often impossible to discover whether the bottle is of value or not.

The two most important ingredients needed to clean freshly dug bottles are patience and elbow grease. A good set of stiff brushes of various sizes will help, too. Any one of a variety of the ammonia-base household cleaners will dissolve the top grime, but usually the only answer for very dirty bottles, particularly those with narrow necks, is several days soaking in a pail of sudsy ammonia and water. It is advisable for anyone working with a strong ammonia solution to wear rubber gloves.

Stronger cleaning solutions, those that contain lye, require special caution when used. The commercial products that are used for opening clogged drains or removing stains from toilet bowls have directions concerning their use on the packages and these should be closely followed. While many of these products will remove stubborn dirt from old bottles, the user should take every precaution not to mix one product with another. Small stones, tacks or any other small hard objects may be rattled around inside a bottle when a brush is not successful in removing dirt that has stuck. One should be careful that whatever hard objects are used, they do not scratch the inner surface of the bottle.

After a thorough soaking in whatever cleaning product one prefers and an extra wash to remove any remaining dirt particles, the bottle should be rinsed in clear water and turned upside down to drain dry. Care should be taken that the bottle is propped in some way so that it does not fall over and break.

Some old bottles have a clouded appearance after they have been washed. This is caused by the oxidization of some of the chemicals in the glass and when this "sick" glass is in an advanced state, nothing can be done to improve its appearance. However, the opalized appearance of "sick" glass *in extremis* is desired by many collectors and the bottle thus found is not necessarily worthless. Extreme examples of "sick" glass is that reclaimed from Greek, Egyptian and Roman ruins and the iridescent pastel colors resulting from centuries of burial are beautiful.

In the case of slightly "sick" glass, which is occasionally found in dug bottles, the first traces of oxidization do little to enhance the appearance of the glass, but give it patches of cloudiness that are somewhat unattractive. Rubbing these spots with clear mineral oil can be at least a temporary cure for this condition.

When the cloudiness is on the inner surface of the bottle any method can be devised to reach this glass in order to apply the oil to the clouded areas. If the oil successfully "erases" the cloudy patches, the bottle can then be corked and it will stay clear for a good length of time. While this is not a cure, it will at least make the bottle more presentable temporarily and the process can be repeated when necessary.

There is no collector of glass bottles who has not suffered a loss when knocking over and breaking a favorite bottle. This can sometimes be avoided by applying a little photographer's adhesive to the bases of flasks and bottles that are wobbly. When a bottle is broken beyond repair, it is best to throw it away and forget about it. The accident has made room for another, perhaps more interesting, bottle. If, as is too seldom the case, the bottle is broken in only a few pieces or, perhaps, slightly chipped or cracked, one must weigh the value of the broken bottle against the effort or expense required to repair or restore it. A neck chip can be ground down, but if the bottle or flask is of value, this is sometimes a risk. Glass can break further during the grinding and polishing process. It is probably better to leave well enough alone, especially in the case of really old bottles that might be irreplaceable.

Cracks in the sides or necks of bottles can be repaired or strengthened by careful application of casting resin, often called "liquid glass." If the contours of the bottles are such that a brush cannot reach the inner surface, then a thin application on the outer surface of the cracked area will at least strengthen the bottle somewhat and help prevent further destruction. Broken bottles may be pieced together by careful use of a new adhesve made for repairing glass and ceramics. Just do not become so absorbed that you forget that broken glass is sharp.

Embossments may be ground off or added to a bottle and the novice collector should be aware of this. Plain bottles can be given embossments through the careful application of molded letters made of resin, thereby fraudulently enhancing the value of an otherwise plain bottle. Whenever any object becomes desirable to collectors, there are always charlatans who will go to great lengths to oblige an eager market by devising methods of supplying these items—or reasonable facsimiles. Color can be given to an existing clear glass bottle and embossments added or deleted, thereby making a silica purse out of a sow's ear for some eager and unsuspecting buyer.

Many of the paper labels found on old bottles can be improved by cleaning and treating them by methods one would use to restore old prints and lithographs—which, indeed, many of the labels are. Most frequently the paper on which these labels were engraved or printed is of a quality that will respond to careful removal from the bottle, washing, and repair. However, manipulation of some paper labels will lead to total disintegration and the more fragile labels or wrappers should be let alone.

Some labels that seem to be of little value as yet may become increasingly important as information concerning their designers and manufacturers comes to light. Paul Revere was an engraver who made trade labels and it is probable that many more important American artists earned a living in this manner.

Most labels will not suffer from a delicate wash of warm soapy water wrung out in a piece of cotton. Further repair or cleaning which results in the removal of the label is not recommended unless the label is in such terrible condition that it will not last otherwise. Any repairs or alterations that are done to any old object should be kept as minimal as possible. As is the case with most antiques and collectible items, excessive restoration decreases rather than enhances the value.

The collection of old bottles as a hobby can be rewarding. There are bottles to fit anyone's purse and for the more ambitious, they are there in the ground waiting to be dug. As manufacturers become more aware of the necessity to reclaim used bottles and many of our familiar glass containers become replaced with plastic, it is today's bottle collectors who will have preserved so much of the history of the development of America's glass industry on their shelves. The hobby of collecting bottles has already enriched the lives of thousands of this generation of Americans. New devotees of old and new glass join the ranks every day. Nowhere in collecting history has there been a pastime that can be so instructive and interesting as the multi-faceted and fascinating hobby of bottle collecting.

Bibliography

Adams, John P. *Bottle Collecting in New England: A Guide to Digging, Identification and Pricing*. Somersworth, New Hampshire: New Hampshire Publishing Company, 1969.

Bartholomew, Ed. *1001 Bitters Bottles*. Fort Davis, Texas: Bartholomew House, 1970.

Burton, John. *Glass: Handblown, Sculptured, Colored; Philosophy and Method*. Philadelphia, Pa.: Chilton Book Company, 1967.

The Corning Glass Center. Corning, New York: Corning Glass Works, 1958.

Davis, Marvin and Helen. *Bottles and Relics*. Medford, Oregon: Grandee Printing Center, Inc., 1970.

Freeman, Larry. *Grand Old American Bottles*. Watkins Glen, New York: Century House, 1964.

Hughes, G. Bernard. *Victorian Pottery and Porcelain*. New York: Macmillan, 1959.

Hunter, Frederick William. *Stiegel Glass*. New York: Dover Publications, Inc., 1950.

Kendrick, Grace. *The Antique Bottle Collector*. Sparks, Nevada: Western Printing and Publishing Company, 1968.

Kroll, Harry Harrison. *Bluegrass, Bells and Bourbon: A Pictorial History of Whiskey in Kentucky*. Cranberry, New Jersey: A. S. Barnes and Company, 1967.

Lord, Francis A. *Civil War Collector's Encyclopedia*. Harrisburg, Pa.: The Stackpole Company, 1963.

McKearin, George S. and Helen. *American Glass*. New York: Crown Publishers, Inc., 1941.
McKearin, Helen. *Bottles, Flasks and Dr. Dyott*. New York: Crown Publishers, Inc., 1970.
McKearin, Helen. *The Story of American Historical Flasks*. Corning, New York: The Corning Museum of Glass, 1953.
McKearin, Helen and George S. *Two Hundred Years of American Blown Glass*. New York: Crown Publishers, Inc., 1949.
Moore. N. Hudson. *Old Glass: European and American*. New York: Tudor Publishing Company, 1935.
Munsey, Cecil. *The Illustrated Guide to Collecting Bottles*. New York: Hawthorne Books, Inc., 1970.
Nelson, Lavinia, and Hurley, Martha. *Old Inks*. Nashua, New Hampshire: Cole Printing Company, 1967.
Ormsbee, Thomas H. *Care and Repair of Antiques*. New York: Grammercy Publishing Company, 1949.
Rogers, Francis, and Beard, Alice. *5000 Years of Glass*. Philadelphia and New York: J. B. Lippincott Company, 1937.
Schwartz, Marvin D. *Collector's Guide to Antique American Glass*. Garden City, New York: Doubleday & Company, 1969.
Shephard, Cecil William. *Wines, Spirits and Liqueurs*. New York: Abelard-Schuman, Ltd., 1959.
Tunis, Edwin. *Colonial Craftsmen and the Beginnings of American Industry*. Cleveland and New York: The World Publishing Company, 1965.
Van Rensselaer, Stephen. *Early American Bottles and Flasks*. Peterborough, New Hampshire: Transcript Printing Company, 1926.
Wagoner, George E. (Editor). *Restoring Antique Bottles*. West Sacramento, California: George E. Wagoner. (no date)
Watkins, Lura Woodside. *The Development of American Glassmaking: An Account of the Fourth Exhibition of National Early American Glass Club*. Boston, Mass.: National Early American Glass Club, 1935.
Wilkinson, O. N. *Old Glass: Manufacture, Styles, Uses*. New York: Philosophical Library, 1968.
Yount, John T. *Bottle Collector's Handbook and Pricing Guide*. San Angelo, Texas: Educator Books, Inc., 1967.

Index

Numbers in *italics* refer to captions

DATE DUE

Feb 8 '72	B53			
Mar 10 '72	B222			
Feb 16 '73	B990			

PRINTED IN U.S.A.